The Pygmy Goat in America
with the Nigerian Dwarf
By Alice Hall

Illustrated By Jamie Smith

Copyright © 1982 by Alice Hall dba Hall Press

ISBN 0-932218-13-X

Library of Congress Catalog Card Number 82-90126

Second Printing, revised, 1992

Published by
Hall Press
P.O. Box 5375
San Bernardino, CA 92412

Printed by
Beacon Printery
Redlands, CA

On the cover is the author in 1985 with her AGS Master Champion, Hallcienda Carlotta, P-427 an early daughter of Ron's Little Carl, page 124.

Foreword

Alice Hall has been raising dairy goats since 1948. In 1961 she established the well-known Hallcienda Nubian Herd, and in 1971, she added a first pair of Pygmies to Hallcienda Farms.

Mrs. Hall has been active in the administration of dairy goat organizations, having served as president of several state associations and three terms on the Board of Directors of the American Dairy Goat Association (nine years). She was also the first vice-president of National Pygmy Goat Association. She is also on the AGS Board.

Mrs. Hall has judged dairy goats in twenty of the United States and in Canada. She has judged as many as twenty-five shows per season, and at the same time, shown her own animals in as many as 12 events each year. She was selected as a classifier for ADGA, and she is a classifier and training chairman for judges of the American Goat Society. She was a judge and certifier for NPGA and AGS, and she has evaluated hundreds of Pygmies in that capacity.

She is a lecturer on dairy goats and has conducted classes on dairy goat management at Crafton Hills College and the University of California at Riverside. Mrs. Hall authored several books, including *Dairy Goats; Selecting, Fitting, Showing*, and *Nubian History; America and Great Britain*. She has also written numerous articles in United Caprine News and Dairy Goat Guide, the AGS Dispatch & Yearbook.

Her experiences in raising, showing, judging, certifying and classifying plus her insatiable appetite for additional knowledge concerning these animals, make Alice Hall a well qualified author for a book such as this. Information contained in it will satisfy a void in the literature on caprine husbandry and will be recommended reading for those interested in the subject.

Robert A. Jackson, DVM

Preface

This book had to be written! Education is my profession, and I had to share what I've learned in the past few years. Hopefully this book will become a part of history--a part that can be updated & be a stepping stone for further research and development of a breed of goat I have come to admire much--the Pygmy.

Eva Rappaport's call to me in 1975 was a real boost of vigor. I'd been breeding Nubians for 14 years. I was winning in almost every show I entered and my Nubians were pace-setters in show and production. I'd been a director for ADGA and judges trainer for AGS. I'd accomplished all I'd set out to do with Hallcienda Nubians, and there was nowhere else to go with them. I was bored, and the Pygmies gave me that new goal I needed.

Being in on the beginning of a new breed, new herdbook, even a new registry was an exciting challenge to me. I'd already had some experience with Pygmies. I'd already met some of the great men at work with the University of Oregon, and I'd visited their Pygmy facility in conjunction with an AGS convention in Portland. I was fascinated with the work that lay ahead.

From the start I was appalled at the extreme emotionalism I encountered in dealing with owners of Pygmies working on the new breed. Everything was taken so personally that it was impossible not to have hurt feelings. Most owners seemed incapable of working with facts--emotions notwithstanding, and it was a real disappointment to me to see the misunderstandings and rifts developing. The split between NPGA and AGS was quite discouraging, and the widening of the gaps is disheartening.

As I've organized facts from my voluminous file of Pygmy material for this book, I've often had to wonder why, if the founders of NPGA didn't think their animals were milk goats, they petitioned the dairy goat registries to work with them. Then it dawned on me that many of the founders did indeed see their animals as milk goats. The drift away from that concept has occurred since then, and it has made a new rift.

But all is not darkness on the Pygmy political front. Emotions seem to be smoothing out, & and gaps that seem great have bridges being built over them. The future of the Pygmy breed can be bright. Pygmy breeders, let's make it that way!

I wish I could share how some of these Pygmy herds got started--how some of these animals were traded, but that has to remain quiet for now, not that silence makes it any less interesting!

I acknowledge special assistance from a very admirable man, Dr. Ralph Bogart, who helped me to learn how to judge the Pygmy and understand something of its genetics.

I acknowledge with much appreciation all the knowledge I acquired from my good friend, Dr. Robert Jackson, who, as our County veterinarian, did keep Hallcienda Farms surviving for twelve years, and I wish him a most joyful retirement.

A special "thank you" to long-time associate in ADGA, Bill Maxwell of Maryland, for sharing so much of his valuable information on early Pygmy importations with which he was involved or in any other way had first-hand knowledge.

I acknowledge the help and support my husband, Roger, has given me in raising Hallcienda animals of all breeds, in goat politics (he served on the AGS Board and as its president during the beginning turmoil of the Pygmy breed), and in encouraging and reviewing this book.

I acknowledge the help of our friends, Loren and Janet Johnson, in encouraging, reviewing, and proofing this book, and I acknowledge the help of my parents, John and Gladys Eby, and a friend, Juli Coughlin, in proofreading.

Thank you all!

Table of Contents

CHAPTER	PAGE
What is a Pygmy?	8
Pygmy Purposes	14
Importations	18
Registries	20
Breed Standards	27
Care and Feeding	32
sanitation	38
hair, hoofs, horns, etc.	42
tattooing, wethering, deodorizing	47
Well Goat/Sick Goat	52
injections and medication	58
Breeding and Kidding	65
Selecting a Good Animal	73
Score Cards and Fitting	84
Sanctioning and Show Classes	94
Showmanship	112
After Show	125
What is a Nigerian Dwarf?	127
Nigerian/Pygmy Comparison	133
Breed Quiz	138
Bibliography	139
Quiz Answers	140

List of Illustrations

Master Champion Hallcienda Carlotta	Cover
Early Does, Pygmy and Dwarf	31
Equipment and Hoof Trimming	43
Tattooers, Dehorners, Elastrators	46
Dehorning and Tattooing	48
Injection Sites	63
Abscesses	64
Delivering a Kid	70
Pygmy Palace Molly and Rose	72
Ideal Pygmy and Parts of Body	74
First Show Champions, Meg and Silver	75
A Poor Pygmy	79
Dual Champion Buck, Taurus	83
Clipping for Show	88-89
Chino Acres Clipped Does	91
AGS Champion, Bearget	99
A Good Producer	103
Happy Easter	105
NPGA Champion, Lisa	109
Circling the Ring	112
Postion of Exhibitors and Judge	113
Setting Up a Doe	115
Moving an Animal into Postition	116
Dual Champion, Billie Jean	118
Moving in Line	120
Leading an Animal and Changing Places	121
Trading Places Side-by-side	122
Walking Side-by-side	123
Ron's Little Carl	124
Two Golden Dwarves	129
A Caramel Dwarf	131
Two Dwarf Bucks	132
A Schwartzhal Dwarf Doe	134
A White Dwarf	135
Dwarf Buck and Doe	137
Breed Picture Quiz	138

What Is a Pygmy ?

In America it's the Pygmy Goat. That's all. It's short and simple that way, and it lacks definition, which is perhaps best when no one seems to be sure what precise animal the United States is dealing with. It is an achondroplastic dwarf. The most prominent goat of this type is the West African Dwarf Goat found in Nigeria, Ghana, & the Cameroons, although similar animals are also seen in Zaire, Angola, Nambia and the Sudan. (8 & 9)

In addition, achondroplastic dwarf goats,(an animal that has a fairly normal trunk and short legs), are seen in India, Nepal, Siberia, Lapland Arabia, Japan, China, Tibet, Malaysia,and the West Indies. (8 & 9) The West African Pygmy, which is also called the Fouta Djallon, Cameroon, Nigerian Dwarf, and tree goat, has had the most research done on it, but almost no pictures of it in Africa are printed. Ethiopia also has a dwarf goat.

Generally, the WAD (West African Dwarf) is described as being 15.4 to 22.6 inches tall with mature weights of 44 to 66 pounds. Actually, the WAD goat is said to come in three classes in its native Nigeria--small, medium and large. Height at withers, body length, depth of side and length of side are the dimensions that determine into which category an African Dwarf falls. Average heights for each category are small--15.4 inches; medium--17.3 inches; large--20.6 inches. (9) The WAD is said to have very short horns (those in Southern Sudan have 2-3 inch horns), and to be seen in all colors and combinations of colors, although agouti is the most common. (8) WAD goats average 1.8 kids per year, and they are used for meat & milk in their native land. (8 & 9)

In fact, values placed on WAD goat milk look

very promising. Compared with Alpine and Saanen milk, the milk of the West African Dwarf shows at least 65% more Calcium, 20% more Phosphorus, about the same amount of Magnesium, 20% less Sodium, a little less Chlorine, about 75% more Potassium, and 35% more iron. WAD milk solids run 17.87-18.68 % compared with the Saanen's 12.24-13.47%. WAD milk usually runs at least 2% higher in butterfat than Saanen milk, and its lactose is almost 1.5% higher. The Dwarf's crude protein is almost one percent higher than the Saanen's milk protein. (9)

In addition to the wide-spread African Dwarf Goat, East Africa has a small goat that does not show the dwarf proportions, but it does stand at 23.62 inches and weighs 55 to 66 pounds. It has one-to ten-inch horns, and it comes in all colors with the "caramel" pattern as described by the NPGA often seen. (8) The East African Small goats come in two varieties with those from Kegezi being more compact than those from Muhende. (8)

The Bengal from India is a 17-30 pound meaty goat that gives from two to six pounds of milk a day. It has short ears and coat, comes in black brown and white, kids twice a year with 60% twins and 10% triplets. (8)

The South China Goat is a meat goat with ears that are short and alert, six- to ten-inch horns, a short black coat, a concave head, disproportionately short legs, and a thickset, muscular body. It commonly has twins. It measures 19.7 to 21.6" at the withers and weighs 55 to 66 pounds. (8)

Just as the rest of the world has so many kinds of Dwarf goats that could fit the USA Pygmy standard, this country has different types in the breed, too. There seem to be at least two types of Pygmies in the U.S.A.--the meatier type which converts excess feed into meat and fat, and dairy type which puts excess feed into the udder & milk pail. These types are not mentioned in literature probably because most goats in other countries do not ever have a chance to be overfed. In fact, a paper from Nigeria states that production of the WAD goat there is very poor at the village level because of the poor feed, which consists of table scraps and natural vegetation. (9) Where a Pygmy in this country can easily weigh 80 pounds, even Pygmies here that are on natural browse weigh 45 to 65 pounds. Feeding makes quite a difference.

One reason the Pygmy in Africa is so prominent compared with the other breeds is because it is resistant to the tse tse fly, which can destroy other breeds of goats. When other animals are imported to Africa, they must often be kept in huts and hand-fed with cut vegetation so they have no contact with the fly.

The Pygmy is a very versatile animal. It is used for milk, meat, hides, and perhaps blood, in Africa. It may have saved the lives of Jews with its milk in Nazi Germany. Rumor has it that the Pygmy was not confiscated with other livestock as the Nazis believed it to be worthless.

In America, the Pygmy has been a zoo novelty, a research animal, and a pet. As its numbers increase and it falls into the hands of people experienced with goats, it is more and more being used for milk and meat, too.

University of Oregon Medical School in Portland, Oregon, probably had the largest, most well known herd of Pygmies for research, but other universities also have used them sporadically. In Oregon, Pygmies were used for studies in fetal physiology and cardiac output during pregnancy and postpartum. Publications from the University say that Pygmies were used because "their small size makes them easy to handle, inexpensive to feed & economical to house. They withstand surgery well under halothane anesthesia and do not 'worry' the surgical wounds." (1)

In addition, University of Oregon states "all individuals in our herd have a single hemoglobin type (defined by stanch-gel electrophoresis) with a single blood-oxygen equilibrium curve, which is a matter of physiologic importance." (2) They say too, that Pygmies are easy to train and heal promptly.(3)Besides all of those advantages,Oregon found their Pygmies to be odorless (except a mature buck), quiet and clean, and they "readily become attached to humans, especially when raised by hand." (3)

In comparing the Pygmy with the other five breeds of goats, the American Goat Society says, "The Pygmy is a milk goat with dwarf-like proportions of short legs, short but large head, and lots of width. The Pygmy is wide between the eyes, in the chest, between the legs. It is shorter and cobbier than the Toggenburg (which is the smallest of the rest of the breeds), and carries more muscling than any other breed. The width and depth of body compared with height are greater than in the other breeds. The eyes are prominent and bright. Light colored Pygmies often have darker legs, dorsal stripe, and martingale, and dark-colored Pygmies often have light etching on the ears, crown, muzzle and eye-rims.The coat is full, heavy and medium-length. All colors are acceptable." (4)

Also in comparing the Pygmy with the Swiss breeds, Oregon says, "Pygmy goats are physiologically more mature at birth than newborn dairy goats." (1) Unschooled breeders may not be able to explain that statement except to say that they have noticed new Pygmy kids to be more active and agile,running faster, bouncing and jumping higher and earlier than kids of other breeds.

Readers have probably already noticed a confusion of terms in referring to Pygmy goats. In some writings they are called "milk goats," even dairy goats, and in other writings they are not classified with the "dairy goats" at all. This is a real and existing conflict--what is the purpose of the Pygmy?

A 1951 publication from England, *The Class-*

ification of West African Livestock, by I.L. Mason, says that the Pygmy goat is "low in milking ability." However, nothing is said about management, and what effect that might have on native animals. And, a 1971 paper from University of Oregon says that "Pygmies have been valuable in varied areas of biomedical research, they are excellent pets, are very useful in contact zoos and mobile animal teaching laboratories, as well as for the more accepted uses, meat and milk..." (1). This controversy over whether or not this breed, the Pygmy, is a dairy goat affects all Pygmy production in the United States today and will be discussed at length.

The Pygmy herd at Oregon was admittedly not necessarily typical of the native African Pygmy herds. The Oregon herd was selected to include, primarily, animals that ranged on the small side. Few of their animals reached the maximum height that they knew existed in Africa. (1)

The genetic work with the Pygmy at University of Oregon revealed that the Pygmy's size is probably controlled by three pairs of genes that may be affected by some modifying genes, the effects of which are not major. These genes are located on the 60 chromosomes (30 pairs) that the goat's cells contain. (This compares with 54 in the sheep, 57 in that occasional sheep-goat cross and 46 in humans).

In the goat, the two major pairs of genes for size are for height & meatiness. The Pygmy is homozygous recessive for small size (ss) and homozygous dominant for meatiness (MM). A Swiss goat is homozygous dominant for large size (SS) and homozygous recessive for lack of meatiness (mm). Probably no Nubians or LaManchas were included in the study, and since their breed phenotypes show more meatiness than the Swiss breeds they will not be discussed here. The third major pair of genes for size seems to lack dominance, so in figuring percentages of probability, the third pair is ignored.

In crossing Pygmy goats with Swiss goats, ssMM x SSmm, the offspring would all be intermediate animals, SsMm, somewhat larger than a Pygmy and somewhat smaller than the Swiss animal. In the second generation, after crossing two of the crossbreds, the projected results would offer, out of 16 kids, nine that could be larger (at least meatier) than the Swiss grandparent, one might be smaller than the Pygmy grandparent, three that would be about the size of the Swiss grandparent and three that would be about the size of Pygmy grandparent.

Just how color is inherited in the goat has not really been established. In most animals a darker color seems to be dominant over the light colors, but the goat seems to be an exception to that. The white, which some theorize might be a mutation, is dominant over all other colors. It may express itself in creams or browns, but that simply means that it is heterozygous (Ww) & not homozygous (WW)--that it carries a color gene in with the white. So the way breeders see it, the white is dominant over red, which is dominant over black. Agouti may be inherited separately & contain expressions in red, tan, & black.

Two black parents usually produce only black although a little chocolate may show up at times. Two agouti parents may produce agouti, black or black and tan offspring. Crossing caramel (white or light with more-or-less standard markings) on agouti usually gives 50% of each in the kids.

Patterns are difficult to predict. Standard on one side and spotted or splashy on the other seems to result in about 50% of each in the kids, but breeding two splashed animals can produce a standard kid, and breeding two standards can result in splashy kids.

It is typical for a Pygmy to look less like a Pygmy as a yearling than any other time. The typical proportions are best seen after the age of four.

Pygmy Purposes

The purpose of the Pygmy goat is very much a matter of debate. Even Pygmy owners and breeders --even Pygmy registries--cannot agree on why people own Pygmies. But then, when the situation is analyzed, the same problem exists with the other breeds of goats, too. The problem lies partly in that most people who own goats of any size have "small (pet) animal attitudes" even though their animals are considered to be large animals or even livestock.

Goats are lovable, so people's emotions tangle up with them as much as they do with dogs or cats. Because of the emotional entanglement, it is hard to see goats as anything other than loving pets. And that they are! They can be house broken. They can be trained to do tricks. They can be taken for walks. Goats can do anything that a pet of any other kind can do.

But goats can be so much more than pets! For one thing, they are edible. Of course, if emotional involvement is there, no one is going to be eating them. But that doesn't change the fact of chevon (goat meat) being very good meat, and that Pygmies, with their tendency toward heavier muscling and "easy keeping" ability make more chevon for their size than most other breeds. Pygmies are almost as much in demand for meat as are the Nubians. Interesting how the African breeds are the meatiest!

Chevon is probably best bar-b-qued. It is sometimes called "Baaa-b-q," and it is good! If a man's Pygmies are pets, it might behoove him not to make pets of young males so that they can be castrated and eaten. That is certainly better for the breed than keeping all males as bucks. They aren't all worthy of being bucks, and those that aren't should be castrated for whatever purpose.

Chevon is also delicious roasted or stewed. It may have a stringier texture than beef, but it is comparable in many other ways. "Prairie rabbit" is also pretty good. If a kid a few days old is dressed out, coated and fried like rabbit, it makes pretty good eating, too, although meat that young does not contain much of the flavor most people are accustomed to.

Chevon is a clean meat because it comes from a clean animal. A person who is squeamish about eating "unclean" animals, certainly has no worry about eating chevon.

Each owner has his own attitudes about eating his goats. Because of emotional involvement some people refuse to eat any chevon. Others will eat wethers raised for that purpose. Some may eat doe kids and wethers. Others will even eat older does and bucks. It's an individual matter, but killing and butchering an animal is not the most cruel thing that can happen to it. Living with an unloving, uncaring, undisciplined family is probably harder on the animal than having its life ended.

Three categories of goats have been defined ie.--milk, meat and hair. It's obvious that the Pygmy is not a "hair goat." Hair goats have an annual shearing, and their wool or cashmere is a commercial product. Obviously, Pygmies do not fit in that category. Pygmies can be categorized as meat goats because they are often well-muscled and carry adequate fat for good meat, but most Pygmy owners don't like to think of their animals in that way.

That leaves milk. Are Pygmies dairy goats? Some people argue that they can't be because of their impracticality in a commercial situation-- but if that's the criterion, it's questionable if there is such a thing as a dairy goat in any of the breeds. Their seasonal breeding tendencies make them impractical commercial animals.

For their size, many Pygmies produce just as efficiently as does of any other breed, but most

Pygmy breeders are not ready to call their goats dairy goats because they are not ready to commit themselves to daily milking procedures. Those who have done so have found that 1) Pygmies will milk almost a full ten months (a complete lactation in a dairy cow) when they are not bred back and when they are milked regularly, twice a day, every day, 2) Pygmies, for their size, produce almost as well as some of the other dairy goats--giving an average of $2-2\frac{1}{2}$ pounds a day (that's over a quart), & 3) the milk is absolutely delicious, running from $3\frac{1}{2}\%$ to $10\frac{1}{2}\%$ butterfat. Most Pygmies seem to be averaging around 6-7% butterfat, and the milk is very sweet.

Corinne Odiorne of the Fortunatus Herd did some of the original work with milk production in Pygmies in the early 1970's. She was selecting a herd for production at that time, and she decided to do this rather than cross-breed for more production. In her early work, she found the crossbreds were not as productive or as stylish as the pure animals of either breed.

Although most Pygmies seem to give $2-2\frac{1}{2}$ lbs. of milk a day, there is an occasional doe giving $4\frac{1}{2}-5$ pounds a day, and one doe is known to have given over six pounds a day. However, that Pygmy doe had been bred to Alpine and LaMancha bucks and may have been influenced by the genetics of the kids she carried through the hormones produced in the placenta. At least that is a theory.

American Goat Society considers the Pygmy a milk goat because its ribs angle toward the rear flank as in a dairy animal rather than running in a strictly vertical fashion as in a meat animal-- and AGS is establishing minimum requirements for Pygmies to earn their production stars. Minimum requirements for Pygmies will probably be set at one-third what is required for the other breeds.

The other major use for Pygmies in America is for research. Their physical and psychological structures make them ideal for research, but since there is no category for "research" goats, since it's still just milk, meat or hair, Pygmy owners will have to define their animals in those terms. Since the Pygmy does an adequate job in two of the established categories, perhaps it is a dual purpose animal.

However, until a breeder defines what he wants his Pygmies to be, his breeding goals will be nebulous. Breeders with nebulous breeding goals can only weaken a breed, so it would be a wise thing for Pygmy breeders in general to agree on the purpose of the Pygmy Goat.

Some breeders are sold on Pygmies as producing dairy animals. One Pygmy breeder had Pygmies on production test with the big breeds. As it was group test, many different people came to do the milk-weighing. One man was a scoffer.

"Really!" he said, "Pygmies on test? That's ridiculous! Why bother with them at all?"

"Weigh the milk," said the owner. And the man was surprised at 2.1 pounds the first milking.

"Now taste the milk," said the owner.

"Never!" said the man. "I hate warm milk!"

But the owner prevailed, and the man drank.

"Mmmmm," he said, handing the glass to his wife, "you have to taste this. It's like drinking a warm milk shake!" And he drained the glass.

"If I were to buy a goat," said he, "I would buy a Pygmy!"

And that man is an excellent judge!

GOOD TASTING MILK IS WHY PYGMIES ARE IN BIOSPHERE II.

Another breeder insists that the Pygmies help her relationship with her in-laws, who would not drink goat milk. Whenever they visited, cow milk would have to be purchased and comments ignored.

"Now that we're milking Pygmies, my in-laws drink the milk! What a relief!"

Importations

Just how the Pygmy arrived in America, or for that matter when, is not actually known. Importers have been bringing animals in from Africa, and perhaps from Asia, illegally as well as legally for a long time. Several excellent herds claim to have a beginning from illegal and unrecorded importations. Apparently, Pygmies are transported from Africa on ships bringing lions over--to feed the lions enroute --and any "leftover" Pygmies are sold when the ship docks in this country. If Pygmies are brought from Africa with lions, why not from Asia with tigers?

By the middle 1930's, Benson's Animal Farm in New Hampshire had Pygmies--mostly agoutis. Consuela Vanderbilt imported Pygmies for her two estates in the 1940's. Many thoroughbred horse breeders were referred to her for companion goats for their horses. Before World War II, the Hagenbach Company of Germany was a primary exporter/collecter of zoo animals and handled a lot of Pygmies. (10)

In 1953 or 1954, Dr. William Mann, director of the National Zoo in Washington, D.C. was instrumental in importing about 60 Pygmy goats that were put on ship in several West African ports and unloaded in Miami, Florida. The shipment was about 80% does; 100% agouti. They were small, young adult Pygmies, with the males measuring about 14 inches at withers and the does being smaller, & all were dehorned. (10)

In 1959, when Sweden was removed from a list of restricted countries due to hoof and mouth disease, Heinz and Lutz Ruhe of Jungleland, California and Mrs. Lindemann of the Catskill Game Farm in New York imported just over a dozen animals from Sweden that had originated in West Africa. The animals in this importation were all of the agouti coloration, as the earlier ones were, and they had the black or black-spotted cannon stockings. (5)

In 1966, Randolph Hearst imported seven Pygmies from the North Coast of the Cameroons in West Africa to run on the pastures of his beautiful and picturesque castle on the California coast. Five of these goats were black. One was agouti, and one was white with black markings. Some had wattles & some did not. The Hearst herd went to the San Diego Zoo when it was disbanded. (10)

After World War II, it took the Hagenbachs a while to get back into business, but it did get several batches of Pygmies into the United States in the late 1940's or early 1950's. This Company also handled the importation for the University of Oregon Medical School. (10)

Most zoos, like most owners, try to keep the Pygmy herds pure, but the belief that it is difficult for Pygmies to breed with the larger breeds has probably had some negative effects on the outcome of that attempt. One can often see bucks of the larger breeds running with a Pygmy herd, and just because he is three times the size of the does doesn't mean he can't breed them. And the Pygmy buck, as little as he is, can work so fast that he can breed a much larger doe on the run and jump if he has to.

This chapter outlines importations that can be documented. There is also conjecture that Pygmies could have come over as early as the slave ships that ran from West Africa. The fact that a lot of "native" American goats show the Pygmy type indicates this may be a possibility. Pygmy type is seen in the Southeastern Hillbilly Goats, the Texas Nervous Goat, one type of "Spanish" goat, and the Catalina Goat, as well as the "native" goats found in Hawaii. Mr. Ruhe supposed (5) that there was a little crossbreeding going on between his imported Pygmies in other herds and these "native" small-type goats, and he concluded that this might not be too bad, since the size was not being enlarged greatly (5).

Registries

By 1972, Pygmy goats were being registered by the Animal Research Foundation in Quinlan, Texas. ARF had been founded by Tom Stodghill for the survival of rare breeds of animals of all kinds, and Ruth Enriquez and Ann Werts of California were instrumental in having Pygmies added to the ARF herd books.

The ARF breed standard for AFRICAN PYGMY GOATS was as follows:

Height: Does not over 22 inches, any height under.

Bucks: not over 24 inches, any height under.

Color: Black, Silver black, or Silver blue in body color.

Ears: Silver and small, ERECT.

Eyes: Silver rings around eyes.

Nose: Silver, may have white spots on head or body, or small amount of white on feet—as long as white doesn't distract from body color. No brown or other color permitted.

The ARF breed standard for AMERICAN PYGMY GOATS, to be registered separately from the African Pygmies, with the requirement that they be at least half Pygmy was:

Height: Does or Bucks not over 25 inches.

Color: Any color permitted.

Any goat that is part Pygmy is to be registered as American Pygmy. (6)

But even with those standards, the ARF was registering in its AFRICAN Pygmy herdbook pure white and pure tan Pygmies long before it got to number 100. American 3/4 Pygmies are also there.

African Pygmy #1 in ARF was a buck, 00 a doe and 001 a buck, all owned by Alan Cory, importer.

In 1975, Eva Rappaport of Oregon started contacting Pygmy owners and breeders about establishing a scientific Pygmy breed standard and starting a bonafide Pygmy Goat Registry. Werts agreed to work with the new group, but Enriques opted to stay with the ARF. The executive committee of the new group was resplendent with knowledgeable people, including many of the researchers who had worked for years with the Oregon research herd.

Both existing registries, American Dairy Goat Association and American Goat Society were approached on a preliminary basis in 1975 about registering Pygmies. ADGA flatly excluded Pygmies as a potential breed in its books, and in addition it made a rule that excluded any part-Pygmy animals from its experimental herdbooks.

However, the consensus of the AGS Board of Directors at that time was that AGS would consider registering Pygmies if:

1) a national club was organized to direct certification of the new breed,
2) the national club elected officers,
3) the national club appointed a committee to work with a like committee from AGS,
4) a closed basic Pygmy circle was established,
5) Pygmy color was further defined,
6) an acceptable breed name was established (there being concern about the use of "American" in the breed name, since "American" generally denotes ADGA animals that have been upgraded from crossbreds.)

So the National Pygmy Goat Association was born in September, 1975, with George Blanks of the University Research team as president, Alice Hall as vice president, Eva Rappaport as secretary, and Betty Coe as treasurer. The executive committee, plus James Metcalfe of the Oregon research team, was appointed to work with the AGS committee composed of Pygmy owners Alice Hall, David Moore and Bill House of California, Beverly Myers of Michigan, and Mrs. George Thornton of Arizona.

Dr. Ralph Bogart of the Oregon Research Team represented NPGA at the 1976 AGS Convention in El Cajon, California. He presented the final NPGA plan to the AGS board, and it was accepted by AGS. In following the six requests from AGS, the NPGA was formed, had elected officers and appointed a committee to work with AGS. The oral definition of Pygmy color was that all colors, solid or with markings, were acceptable in the Pygmy breed standard. And the word American was dropped from the name, so the new breed would be simply called "Pygmy."

On the basis of those five requirements, the AGS Board waived requirement #4 for a closed basic Pygmy circle on the basis that the circle would be closed as animals were registered, since no animal would be accepted except by the evaluation of the NPGA certification committee, and since certification would be completed by December 31, 1978.

So on July 31, 1976, the AGS Board passed a motion that "AGS start registering Pygmies as they are certified (by NPGA): that the herdbooks close to new additions as of December 31, 1978; & that Pygmy shows be initiated after the judges' training school of 1977."

However, thirteen Pygmies were included, on a trial basis, in the 1976 AGS judges' training school to demonstrate how the existing AGS score card could be used on Pygmies. The experiment-demonstration went well, and the two Pygmy judges, Bogart and Hall, were able to agree entirely on the placings of the Pygmies.

By September, 1976, the first Pygmies were registered in American Goat Society on the recommendation of the NPGA certification committee, & Eva Rappaport owned the first three Pygmies registered in AGS.

The decision of the AGS Board of Directors to register Pygmies was not unanimous. Carl Romer and Beverly Myers (a Pygmy breeder) voted against it because they were in favor of waiting until the requirement for a basic closed Pygmy circle was completed as originally requested. If the entire board had gone that direction, perhaps a lot of problems would have been avoided--or perhaps a lot of beautiful Pygmies would have been excluded from the herdbooks.

There were problems even before AGS took the vote to register Pygmies. Letters dated November and December, 1975, indicate that NPGA was determined to set policy for AGS, and AGS was just as determined to make its own policies. Neither of the committees appointed to make policies was being consulted, according to these letters, and a few of the officers were doing all the work. Many hard feelings were created. There seemed to be a lack of definition of what the clubs were trying to accomplish--locate animals that fit the standard, or identify purity of breed with one particular importation.

Unfortunately, the situation never improved. Issues became more and more emotional -- especially on the NPGA Board, and NPGA officers were being removed from control either by elimination or resignation, one after another. By the time the AGS convention convened in Oklahoma in 1978, almost an entire new Board with new attitudes was in charge of NPGA, and things were serious. NPGA Board meetings were held in conjunction with the AGS convention, as was a Pygmy show. Many NPGA members were vociferous in objecting to the animals that did not conform to their color standards (which AGS had been assured were only guidelines), but color was not the only problem that surfaced. Both organizations were concerned about basic agreement on the purpose of the Pygmy goat, and, in addition, NPGA didn't like uncertified Pygmies being shown while certification was still in progress. NPGA wanted some involvement in the classification program, & AGS didn't feel that a program that had been functioning well for them for over 30 years should be tampered with by any other organization. The AGS policy of recommending, but not requiring tattoos for registration was objected to by NPGA. NPGA wanted to talk about a possible future reopening of the herdbooks, and since the AGS constitution specifies that all herdbooks were closed, there was real conflict there. NPGA also wanted "privileged use" of the word "Pygmy," and AGS felt that it had a right to use the term, too. In addition to all that, the NPGA Board voiced apprehension about what they would do when they no longer had control over the Pygmy herdbooks. They did not like the idea of being "only a breed club" when the herdbooks closed in AGS in 17 months.

By September, 1978, NPGA members had received a referendum from the NPGA Board to vote on splitting from AGS. Because of considerable confusion on that referendum, it did not pass, and at the December 3, 1978 NPGA Board meeting in Oregon, a little headway was made toward reconciliation.

The meeting was productive, and the face-to-face confrontations seemed to quell the restlessness of NPGA, but it was too late. Absentee board members, in letters following the meetings, were distressing, and in 1979, NPGA did split from AGS. Because AGS chose to continue registering Pygmies, Pygmy breeders now had a choice of three registries. Because so much time was lost in the turmoil, the closing date for herdbooks in both AGS and NPGA was extended at least another year.

In setting up its own certification program, AGS followed the procedures used by NPGA, and two of the original NPGA certifiers, Alice Hall and Max Peabody, went with AGS. AGS defined the purpose of Pygmy registration as being to "record typical animals of the Pygmy type regardless of importation or African background. The purpose is not to immortalize any particular type of Pygmy goat found in Africa, since (many types) may have already been imported into this country." The AGS went further to define the Pygmy Goat as "an unusually small milk goat often showing such dwarf-like proportions as very short legs, large head, large abdomen. It shows its dairy character in its angularity, large barrel, rear-angled ribbing, and often in good udder development, even if it lacks the length of bone and refinement sometimes found in other breeds." (7)

AGS officially closed its herdbooks to new entries December 31, 1979, although some exceptions continued to be accepted, and NPGA closed its herdbooks December 31, 1980. Both registries continued the Progeny testing program for another year or two after herdbook closing date.

Progeny testing was one way a Pygmy could be allowed into the herdbook. An animal was accepted on its own merits if it met the standard for height, cannon length, and proportions, AND if its parents and grandparents also did. It was up to the certification committee to make these judgments based on pictures and pedigree information sent in by the owner/breeder. AGS also allowed personal inspection by one or two certifiers in lieu of the complement of four pictures of each animal required when animals were certified by mail. Animals certified in person were required to file only one photograph.

If the animal was of unknown ancestry, or if parents and grandparents had no measurements taken, but if that animal did meet the standard, it was accepted on "delayed" status. That meant the animal met the standard itself and could be admitted into the herdbooks IF its offspring also met the standard. Animals on delayed status were not allowed into the herdbooks until progeny from them reached the age of six months and could be measured. A buck needed at least eight kids out of at least four does in order to qualify. A doe needed two kiddings by two sires to qualify, and all kids submitted had to meet the standard. The chart printed with the breed standard information on page 30, was developed by the Oregon Research team and shows why the age of six months was established as being the minimum for measurement in certification of progeny for testing of animals on delayed status. However, it was discovered in the course of certification that different lines of Pygmies develop at different rates, and many Pygmies that were over-sized or under-sized when they were six or even twelve months were acceptable for registration when they were mature.

In 1980, due to a disagreement in AGS about fees and timetables for registering animals to be exported, a split resulted in the formation of the International Dairy Goat Registry. IDGR established herdbooks for all six known breeds, and in addition it opened a book for "Nigerian Dwarfs." IDGR is accepting Pygmies from either NPGA or AGS and the herdbooks are open to imports as well as to Pygmies from the other two registries. Open herdbooks never yield a solid seed stock.

IDGR has no standard for the Nigerian Dwarf, but it is registering them in a herdbook separate from the Pygmies on the word of the breeders that the animals are Nigerian Dwarfs. Generally, the Nigerian Dwarfs are described as being smaller & more refined than the Pygmies, but like the Pygmies they come in all colors, with brown being a common one. Nigerian Dwarfs 1-5 in IDGR belong to the Robert Johnson family of Georgia. IDGR & the breeders do not want to set a standard or have the books closed until they accumulate more data on the animals from their native land. They feel that AGS and NPGA have been too rigid, although a lot of the questions these people are raising were presented by AGS before NPGA pulled away, and AGS is probably a lot less rigid than NPGA, even with its closed herdbooks.

So whatever the rationale behind all of this paper work, it does leave Pygmy breeders with a choice of four ways to register--ARF and IDGR for open herd books and AGS and NPGA with closed herd books. In fact, NPGA & AGS herdbooks are so closed that they won't even accept each others' animals.

Breed Standards

The original Pygmy Breed Standard was drawn up by National Pygmy Goat Association and dated May 1, 1975. It was presented to the American Goat Society, which accepted the standard as it was presented in July, 1975. Essentially there have been no changes made in the Pygmy standard by AGS since then, except to revise the wording in the color section, April 24, 1976 to clarify it after a problem arose in this area with NPGA. The NPGA Standard was revised for the same reason in October, 1979.

The Pygmy Goat Standard is printed here in its entirety--indicating where the two standards may differ.

I. GENERAL APPEARANCE (both standards are identical): The Pygmy Goat is genetically small, cobby, compact. Its frame is clearly defined & well angulated; limbs and head are short, relative to body length. Full-barrelled and well-muscled, the body circumference in relation to height and weight is proportionately greater than that of the other breeds. The Pygmy Goat is hardy, alert and animated, good-natured and gregarious.

II. BREED CHARACTERISTICS: Coat (both standards identical)--the full coat of straight, medium-long hair varies in density with seasons and climates. On females, beards may be non-existent or sparce or trimmed; on males, abundant hair growth is desirable; the beard to be full, long, and flowing, the copious mane draping cape-like across the shoulders.

Color--AGS says all colors are acceptable. NPGA says that all BODY colors are acceptable, & they both describe the predominant coloration as the grizzled or agouti pattern. This salt and pepper appearance is produced by the intermingling of light and dark hairs (NPGA adds 'of any color'). AGS adds "Black is also common."

AGS describes "the predominant breed-specific markings include (on black animals) white or light muzzle, forehead, eyes and ears, and (on light animals) black or dark hoofs and cannons, (socks),crown,dorsal stripe, or martingale. Random markings are acceptable."

NPGA describes the same breed-specific markings but says that they are required, so NPGA animals must have markings,whereas AGS will register plain, unmarked animals. NPGA further defines random or optional markings as being light markings on a dark background that appear to be a complete or partial girth belt. " All other patches are seriously faulted" in NPGA.

Both registries are in agreement with the rest of the standard.

Head--short to medium long; profile somewhat dished. Muzzle rounded, not snipey; nose short, wide, flat. Chin and under-jaw full;bite even, neither over nor undershot; jaws broad, strong, well-muscled. Forehead broad, flat or concave. Eyes set well apart,bright, dark, prominent but not protruding. Ears medium-sized & firm, erect, alertly mobile. Genetically horned; disbudding and dehorning permissible.

Neck--well-muscled; shorter, rounder, more full-throated than other breeds; more slender in females than in males.

Shoulder--muscular, well-angulated and well attached; point of shoulder placed posterior to the prosternum (behind the point of the breast bone).

Back--strong, laterally straight, level along chine and loin, rising slightly toward the iliac crest (hip bone).

Loin--broad, strong, nearly level.

Rump--medium long,medium wide, neither level or steep.

Hips--wide, nearly level with back;

Thurls--high, wide apart;
Pin bones--wide apart, somewhat lower than hips, pronounced;
Tail--set high,wide at the base,symmetrical, carried high.
Legs--strong, well-muscled, wide-apart.
Forelegs--short,straight, wide apart,squarely set with elbows close to the ribs; cannon bone short.
Rear legs--when viewed from the rear; straight, widely set to accommodate large barrel; femur and tibia proportionately longer than in other breeds and angulated toward a more pronounced stifle joint,thus compensating for the short hock(or rear cannon). Bone flat and flinty.
Hocks--cleanly molded, sharply angled; metatarsus short. Metatarsus is cannon.
Pasterns--short, strong, and resilient.
Feet--well-shaped, proportioned to size of animal; deep heel and level sole; hoofs symmetrical.

III. DAIRY CHARACTER--animation, agility,general openess. Withers nearly level with dorsal process of the vertebrae. Ribs wide apart, well-sprung, rib bone long, wide, flat. Flank deep, set low on barrel, well-defined. Thighs--long and wide,well muscled; incurving toward udder. Skin--firm, and fine-textured. NPGA adds clean and resilient.

IV. BODY CAPACITY: large in proportion to size of animal,providing ample digestive and reproductive capacity as well as strength,vigor and stamina. Barrel--broad, deep, increasing in width toward flank, thus giving an impression of perpetual pregnancy; symmetrical, well-supported by firm abdominal wall and well-sprung ribs. The disproportionately large circumference of the paunch is greater in females than in males. Heart girth -- large, resulting from long, well-sprung fore ribs; wide chest floor, full at point of elbow.

V. MAMMARY SYSTEM: Udder--firm, rounded, small to medium-sized. Rear attachment--high, halves evenly balanced, symmetrical. Fore-attachment--well forward, tightly attached, without pocket,& blending smoothly into body. Texture-- silky--smooth, elastic, pliable but firm; free of lumps or scar tissue. Teats--cylindrical, of uniform length and size--sufficient for milking with two fingers and thumb; symmetrical placement; free from obstruction, multiple or deformed teats or multiple orifices.

VI. REPRODUCTIVE SYSTEM (BUCKS)--NPGA ONLY: "Testicles--two fully descended, of fairly equal size, healthy and firm. Teats--two non-functional."

VII. BREED SPECIFICATIONS: (The chart below was developed by the Oregon Research team and was to be used for certifying Pygmies for registration. However, experience has shown that not all Pygmies follow this particular growth pattern. Some gain their height at an earlier age, stop growing sooner, and fill out later.)

AGE	SEX	PART	MINIMUM	MAXIMUM	AVERAGE
½yr.	♂	wither	14.17"	19.68"	16.92"
½yr.	♀	wither	12.99"	18.5"	15.74"
½yr.	♂	cannon	2.48"	3.22"	2.87"
½ yr.	♀	cannon	2.36"	3.07"	2.83"
1 yr.	♂	wither	14.56"	19.68"	17.12"
1 yr.	♀	wither	13.77"	18.9"	16.33"
1 yr.	♂	cannon	3.26"	4.4"	3.81"
1 yr.	♀	cannon	3.26"	4.25"	3.74"
Adult	♂	wither	16.0"	23.6"	19.8"
Adult	♀	wither	16.0"	22.4"	19.2"
Adult	♂	cannon	3.7"	4.6"	4.1"
Adult	♀	cannon	3.7"	4.5"	4.1"

Norshaam Sandra Claus, above, an early NPGA/AGS doe bred and owned by Ron Maahs, is pictured as an 18.5 inch, 67-pound yearling, producing five pounds of milk a day on official test at 8-10% butterfat. She didn't show well because extra feed went into milk instead of conditioning. Sandra's line stayed in AGS.

Bonnie Abrahamson's Daisy, another doe of that era is owned by Robert Johnson. She went into the IDGR Dwarf herdbooks and is the oldest Dwarf doe alive at eighteen. She is out of an import doe and is pictured here at age 10.

Care & Feeding

The papers from Oregon say that Pygmies are easy to train and attach themselves to humans. A person who has met a Pygmy will find these statements to be understatements. Anyone who has met a Pygmy has probably fallen in love with that breed. The Pygmy is one capricious caprine! If a Pygmy can't bring laughter, gaiety and enjoyment into a life, nothing can. So people do buy Pygmies.

Then what? People have these loveable and adorable little animals in their homes, but they find they can't quite be raised like a dog, so what do they do with them? Even though a Pygmy can be housebroken and raised like a pet should be, there are many differences in feeding, care and management.

FEEDING

A Pygmy is a goat! Unfortunately, nutrtional standards for any kind of goat have not been officially set. What works well in one part of the country or in one part of the world, or even in one herd, can be completely disproven in any different herd or area. But there are some general rules that can be set down for the care of the Pygmy goat. Here's why!

THE RUMEN

Pygmies are ruminants. That is, they have four compartments to their stomachs. The largest compartment, the rumen, is a fermentation vat in which bacteria and other microflora break down foods into acids, which the animal uses for energy. That's a simplified, incomplete explanation, but it will suffice for starters. The food in the rumen may not be chewed. The micro-organisms work on the smaller food they can handle, &

the rest is burped up in small portions called a cud, to be chewed later. When the cud is reswallowed, it goes to a different part of the rumen, where different micro-organisms work. The rumen is always in a delicate balance between the right number of micro-organisms and the right amount of acid. If either one becomes unbalanced, the goat gets sick, and a ruminant with a stomach ache is a pretty sick animal! That rumen is a LARGE organ. And the rumen in a goat is proportionately larger than the rumen in other ruminants--cows, & sheep and deer.

AMOUNT OF FEED

Because of that larger rumen, the goat probably needs more minerals and more roughage than other ruminants. Half to two-thirds of the goat's diet should be roughage and not more than 80% of the roughage should be a legume (alfalfa, clover, etc.) Some people feed no legume roughage, & the animals do fairly well. Alfalfa is a very rich source of calcium, but the level of calcium in an alfalfa diet is so much higher than the phosphorus level, that arthritis can become a problem. The ideal calcium-phosphorus ratio in a diet is 2:1, but that is almost impossible to meet in a full alfalfa diet, as the calcium-phosphorus ratio in alfalfa is about 17:1. With an alfalfa diet, an awful lot of concentrates (grain) will have to be used to bring the ratio to resemble what it should. On the other hand, a diet too rich in concentrate can predispose an animal to lactic acidosis--high acid condition in the rumen that is often fatal. A good mixture of grass and legume hay is a good diet because legume hay is low in energy and high in minerals, and grasses are high in fiber & low in minerals.

There are three ways to feed a Pygmy-- three rations for animals in different stages of productivity. The three rations are for maintenance, food processing, and food quality. A non-producing animal needs only a maintenance ration if the growth has already been established. A maintenance diet usually means just hay, if that hay can be fairly well balanced in the calcium-phosphorus ratio. A producing animal needs food for maintenance plus a ration for food production (even if a doe is just nursing kids), and a ration for putting nutrients in the food she is producing.

A growing kid is a different story. A baby should have milk for at least six weeks. Two or three months would be better. When the kid has been weaned, it will have to have a high-protein grain in its diet, as well as the high-protein & high energy hay. If the kid has been bred young the protein becomes even more important. On the other hand, high protein diets in mature animals, especially those that are producing, can keep the animals from acquiring the "finish" so important to the show. High carbohydrate puts on flesh.

A general rule of thumb is to feed a mature animal about five pounds of DRY feed for each 100 pounds of body weight (a mature Pygmy doe may be between 65 and 85 pounds, and bucks may be more). Pygmy does in production should have about a half a pound to a pound of grain a day split in two equal portions--one at each milking time. A goat should never be fed according to how much feed is being wasted on the assumption that if feed is being wasted, the animal is getting plenty. Goats are generally wasteful animals, so the solution is to feed in a feeder that prevents as much waste as possible. A "V"-shaped feeder constructed of two-inch welded wire makes a good feeder if the ends are filled in and if a platform is under the "V" to catch waste leaves.

The goat should have a diet that is well-balanced between fiber, protein, fat, and carbohydrates (energy). A well-balanced diet will create a consistent release of energy for general well-being of the animal. Generally, diet should probably include about 17% crude fiber, 14-15% of protein (if 80% of that is digestible), 3-4½% fat and 63-66% carbohydrate.

Many Pygmy owners simply use an alfalfa and grain pellet for the entire ration of the animal. The nutritional value may be correct, but people who feed this way are overlooking the necessity of putting heavy roughage into a rumen that has a need for heavy roughage. University of Oregon used the pelleted feed plus straw. Grass hay is also a good choice, but the goats need a heavy roughage in addition to the pellets if they are used. Pellets have been implicated in aggravating a condition called fat fanerosis or fatty necrosis--a disease much like diabetes that can be treated dietetically.

ROUGHAGE
Pygmies are very efficient browsers and even grazers. In Africa, their native land, they are often called "tree goats," because they climb low-growing and angled trees to browse on branches and leaves. Because Pygmies are short-legged and short-necked compared with other breeds, they are more likely to graze on grass than the larger goats. And because Pygmies are generally "easy keepers," they do well foraging for themselves. If a person has enough land to allow a practice like this, it is an ideal way to keep a herd of Pygmies. Pygmies on good graze and browse need little supplemental hay, although a little alfalfa isn't a bad idea. And, of course some grain at milking time is advised. Little kids should probably not be allowed out to pasture because they are so vulnerable to all kinds of predators. So mothers with little kids may be left penned and fed hay.

Selecting a legume hay is important. Hay should be baled tightly. It should have had a good sun-cure so that it is very dry and unable to mold. However, it should look green and smell sweet. Usually the leaves contain more protein and vitamins than the stems. Hay that contains less than 40% of the original green color probably has a decrease in Vitamin A content of 90%.

Late-cut hays have lower protein. Rains on dry hay cause a loss of 40-60% of the original feed value. That is why hay should be stored carefully.

CONCENTRATES

Pygmies that are not producing milk don't need grain if they have roughage other than alfalfa, along with their alfalfa. Pygmies that are producing milk, even if it's just to feed a kid or two, should have some grain to help increase production. The general rule is that high roughage increases butterfat, and a heavy grain diet increases production. Pregnant Pygmies must not be given a lot of grain. Grain increases an animal's weight when she's not in production, and a fat Pygmy can have a lot of kidding problems. Grain should be added to the diet a couple weeks before kidding, with the amount being increased each day, so that when the doe kids she won't be shocked by sudden addition of grain for production. Sudden addition of grain is a sure way to cause deadly acidosis or founder.

MINERALS

Besides having a larger rumen for her size, the goat has a larger thyroid gland, and for that reason needs more iodine than might be expected. The addition of organic iodine (according to the instructions on the package) to a loose mineralized salt mix is one good way to help a goat get enough iodine. In addition, organic iodine may help prevent foot rot, control abscesses, and it often increases the effectiveness of antibiotic.

A goat needs plenty of calcium and phosphorus in the right proportions, but even then problems may occur. Calcium and phosphorus must be together to make strong bones, but they also need Vitamin D in order to combine. And even then the work can't be done unless magnesium, a trace mineral, is present. If leg or bone problems are evident in a herd, there are four ways to look--calcium, phosphorus, Vitamin D and magnesium. A working combination like this is common in a goat. Mineral trays are becoming popular among goat owners. With this arrangement, the animals may eat whatever minerals their bodies seem to be craving at that time. Goats on browse seldom need such a sophisticated offering, since they can eat plants as they need what those plants offer.

VITAMINS

The goat synthesizes (makes) its own vitamin K and most of the B complex, but Vitamin D is not made. It is not injested either, and in areas of scarce sunlight, a herdsman may have to give Vitamin A,D,E injections at least annually, in the winter.

Vitamin A may also have to be injected when skin problems are evident or when a herd is fighting coccidiosis. Vitamin E is tied with the mineral Selenium in the prevention of White Muscle Disease. Medications such as Bo-Se are often used at least once a year by breeders who want to be sure their animals don't have Selenium deficiency.

Vitamin B, which a goat should make for itself, works with the important mineral, iron, and the trace minerals copper and cobalt to prevent anemia. If an animal shows symptoms of anemia (in pale eye lids) or rough hair coat, the four - way combination of iron, Vitamin D, copper and cobalt, should be checked. If checking can't be done, an injection of crude liver will probably help the animal overcome the symptoms.

Salt is an important mineral for goats, too. A producing doe may excrete an ounce of salt for every gallon of milk she produces, and this must be replaced. Few Pygmies will be losing as much as an ounce every other day but it is essential to replace that salt and provide other salt needs. A container of loose salt allows more ease to goats to pick up the quantity of salt they need, but for the reason of not needing a container, most goat owners still prefer using a salt block. Loose salt is also easier to mix with other minerals, such as organic iodine, but some blocks also have essential minerals, such as Selenium, added.

WATER

Water is a vital consideration. Plenty of it should be available, and it should be pure & clean. Cool water is best. Warm water should be used only if the animals are on limited roughage for some reason. Goats manufacture heat when roughage is digested, so cool water in a full rumen is fine. If the rumen is not so full, warm water may help. It is possible to with-hold water to help a doe to put on flesh or dry off, but it must be done with lots of caution.

A goat's body is over 80% water. Water loss to remove body wastes is heavy, and a 20% loss of water is fatal, so plenty of water should be available at all times for all goats. Since goats are so fastidious, clean water is essential. Self-waterers are good because the animal can always help itself to what it needs to keep water intake above the level of water outflow.

FEED SANITATION

Micro-organisms in the water, or water contaminated by carrier animals in the herd is a serious problem. Water that looks, smells or feels dirty should not be used. Water full of algae shouldn't be offered to animals. The water container should be washed at least weekly, and often with chlorine.

Goats cannot be fed on the ground. They eat a 15% wider selection of roughage plants than other domestic ruminants, but they are far more selective than other animals when it comes to cleanliness of the food they eat. Feed on the ground, besides not being palatable, is a good way to spread disease organisms in the herd. Feed should be in kid-proof feeders at least twelve inches high. All feeders for hay and grain should be constructed of an easy-to-clean material, preferably metal. Wood is too difficult to clean to make it good for feeders.

HOUSING

Goats all dislike being wet, and goats all react with illness to being drafty, so goat housing must offer the animals protection from wind and rain. Housing does not need to be elaborate, especially in mild climates. Three-sided sheds--the open side away from the prevailing cold winds work well in mild climates. Closed barns may be necessary in climates where winter hits hard. In some northern states, animals are completely closed in for six months of the year. If animals in the north are so housed, they must have adequate ventilation through windows placed well above the animals' heads to prevent ammonia-inhalation pneumonia.

If barns are constructed of wood, it may be necessary to cover the lower four feet or so with sheet metal or some material that will keep animals from chewing the barn excessively. Any painting that is done should be done with a non-toxic paint.

Goats are happiest if they have lots of room in which to run and jump. If space is limited, a recommendation from University of Oregon suggests at least ten square feet of indoor space per animal and 20 square feet of outdoor space with boxes platforms, rocks, stairs, and other play equipment to encourage exercise and inhibit obesity. (3) If part of this equipment for play includes a stanchion, the animals can be trained to stand on one for feeding, milking, hoof trimming, hair cutting or injections or other routine grooming.

SANITATION

Sanitation is a means of preserving health or removing or neutralizing elements that injure the health of the animals. Sanitation is the single most important disease opponent or health proponent. Anything that relates to environmental sanitation will help prevent disease in animals.

Sanitation in feeding is vital. Feeders are to be constructed to keep the feed at least high enough off the ground so the animals cannot eliminate into them. Separate creep feeders for kids are good so kids don't have to compete with larger animals for feed, and they MAY help keep kids out of the mature animals' feed.

Wood absorbs moisture and disease-producing bacteria, and it can harbor common toxic molds & even ticks. When possible, feeders for goats are best constructed of metal or concrete so they can be easily cleaned, and they should be cleaned often.

Feed must be stored sanitarily. Bins used for grain storage or pellets should be kept dry & rodent free, and they should be sterilized before use with lime, white wash, formaldehyde or saponified lye. Unslaked lime may also deter rodents. Rodents can easily contaminate feed with Leptospirosis, plague, parasite plague, or Pasturella. Feed stored in bins must have some ventilation-- contact with circulating air and sunlight--or the feed may decompose, or molds or fungi may become toxic, or Clostridium bacteria may be encouraged to grow. Feed must also be stored in a way that will preserve palatability.

Hay must be stored in covered stacks or sheds because bleaching from the sun or soaking by rain both decrease food value. It is ideal to keep hay from rodents, too, but use of rodenticides on or near the bottom layers could lead to contamination of the entire hay supply.

Clean water is essential. Most viruses and many pathogenic bacteria thrive in water, as do a lot of the parasites. If the source of water is questionable, water may be sterilized by boiling, or it may be disinfected by adding chlorine or iodine. Both chlorine and iodine can lose their effectiveness if they are contaminated with organic material, but both can be effective if the source is clean. Chlorine or a halogen can be used in amounts as low as one part per million, and iodine may be used at the rate of one drop per quart or one teaspoonful of Lugol's per fifty gallons.

Algae should be controlled because it interferes with digestion. Algae do not grow as well in fiberglass containers. A wash of copper sulfate will also control algae, but it is not palatable, and it may even be harmful if it is consumed.

Chlorine (one part per million), or iodine, (one to five ppm) or copper sulfate (if washed out thoroughly) may be used to clean water containers. Animals are highly susceptible to copper poisoning, especially in areas where molybdenum is not abundant, so copper containers are never to be used for watering animals. Copper pipes should probably not be used either.

Sanitation in housing is also important, especially at kidding time. The sheds or barns should be exposed to sunlight at least part of the time. Bedding may be straw, shavings, sawdust or sand, but it must be removed & replaced regularly. Straw is least desirable in weather or climates that are damp. Flooring is not too important if it is kept clean. Since wood is so hard to clean, it is probably least desirable for flooring.

Crowded housing is always bad. It has been estimated that as the number of animals doubles, the incidence of disease and parasitism quadruples in a given area.

Sanitation in milking is especially important. It is best to milk on stanchions and in a building with hard-surfaced floors and walls as asphalt, plastic, concrete, so they may be easily washed. Cresylic acid or detergent and water under high pressure are good washing substances, but use of much water requires a good gutter system.

Milking animals should be brushed before each milking to keep loose hair from falling in the milk. Very few Pygmies have hair long enough to require a dairy clip, but that would be good on very long-haired animals. In a dairy clip, a very short cut is given the hair on the tail, on the flanks, thighs and udder.

Udders should be washed and DRIED before a milking. Hands should be washed and DRIED before milking each animal. If kids are not nursing, a teat dip should be used after each milking.

All milking equipment (buckets, strainers, containers) should be stainless steel or glass, or some other material that can be easily cleaned and sanitized. Plastic is not a good material to use for milk. It absorbs odors and flavors and it absorbs butterfat.

A good, fast way to cool milk is essential. Goat milk is delicious when it is handled properly, and Pygmy milk is exquisite. But animals must be fed properly and the milk handled well from start to finish in order to have a high-quality product.

For best sanitation, pens should have solid surfaces that can be scraped and cleaned on a regular basis. Pens should be sloped for good drainage, and there should be isolation areas as far from the main housing area as possible to isolate new animals coming into the herd.

Pasturing is a good way to supplement diets and give animals exercise, but pastures must be rotated to break the parasite cycles. Clean feed and water utensils raised high enough to avoid fecal contamination are a must. Daily removal of manure and bedding is essential in small pens. It is less frequently necessary if the pens are of adequate or large size.

Poor sanitation practices that most often lead to illness in animals include accumulation of manure and urine, too many animals in an enclosure too small, feeding on the ground, water troughs too low, leaking water troughs, lack of sunlight, and poor drainage.

HAIR CARE

Regular inspection of skin and coat, and a program of regular hair brushing are good ways to stay on top of any problem with fleas, ticks or

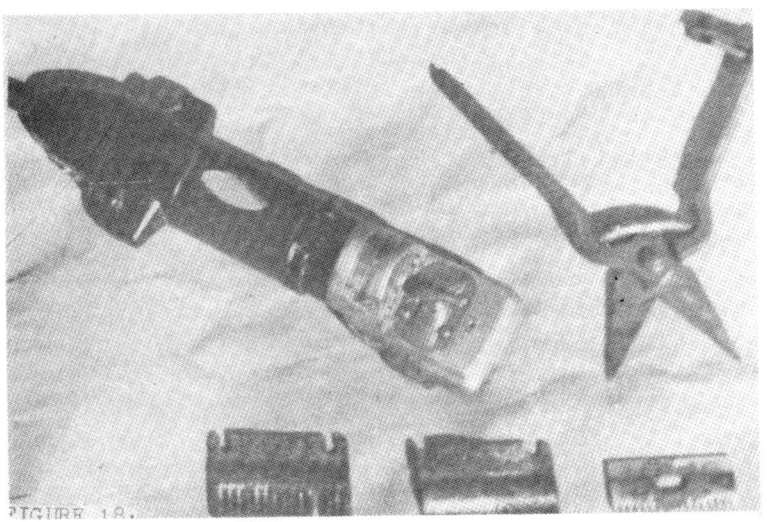

LEFT--HAIR CLIPPERS: RIGHT--GOOD HOOF TRIMMERS
FOREGROUND--PLUCKING, FINE & CUTTING BLADES FOR
HAIR CLIPPERS

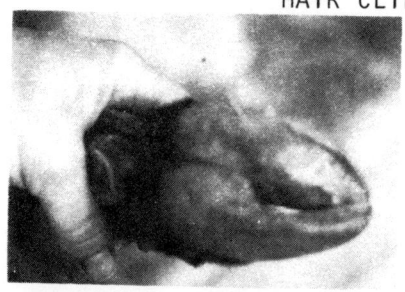
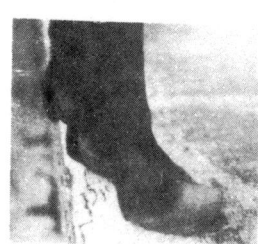
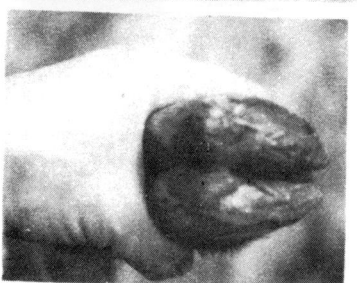
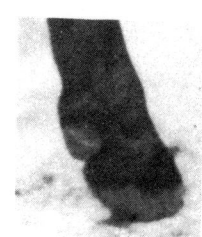

PYGMIES SELDOM HAVE HOOFS THIS BAD, BUT EVEN HOOFS
THIS BAD (TOP) CAN BE CORRECTED BY TRIMMING (BOT.)

mites. These practices will also reveal which animals have problems with pox and other sores. An annual clipping of the hair, especially in spring if the animals have been close-housed all winter, is a good way to control these external parasites, too. Bathing is not a favorite experience for any goat, especially Pygmies, but it is not usually a necessary experience. Bathing may be necessary in cases of serious skin problems, but then it should be done carefully and cautiously so the animal is not chilled. Chilling leads to pneumonia. Use of oil on the hair is not usually necessary either. A goat in good health will have glossy hair. If the hair becomes brittle, it could be a sign that the animal is not properly synthesizing Vitamin B, and therapy with that vitamin might be called for.

HOOF TRIMMING

Pygmy hoofs do not seem to grow as fast as the hoofs of other breeds, and Pygmies seem to be endowed with a more ideally square hoof than are the other breeds. However, Pygmies also tend to have splayed hoofs more than the other breeds do (that helps them climb), and this fault may have to be corrected, when possible, during hoof trimming. An active Pygmy that is on browse, pasture and rocky soil may not have to have hoofs trimmed very often. Pygmies that are housed in small pens with nothing abrasive to climb on, may need to have hoofs trimmed as often as once a month.

Animals must stand squarely and flat on well-trimmed hoofs, or they will acquire serious lameness problems. Hoofs should be trimmed flat all the way round, including the sole and heel. A start at the rear of the hoof may help the husbandman to square things up more evenly. Knives or clippers or rasps or files may be used to trim hoofs. Care must always be taken not to cut so deep that hemorrhage is started. When the germinal epithelium, new skin, of the hoof has been cut, excessive blood may be seen flowing because the blood of the hoof is stored in the lamina at the top of the hoof, &

there are no blood vessels to lacerate to stop the bleeding. Hoofs should be trimmed parallel with the growth rings that can be seen around the outside of each hoof.

DEHORNING

There is no prejudice against Pygmies with a natural set of horns, so whether a Pygmy is horned or dehorned is entirely the decision, based on personal preference, of the owner. All the larger breeds must be dehorned because of the damage they do to one another with horns. Pygmies are so low to the ground that, even though they fight very aggressively, they seldom do the kind of damage to an udder or to testicles that the larger goats do with horns. Pygmies must never be naturally hornless!

Herds that run on browse or graze, and herds that have large pens, probably should be left with horns. Even though Pygmies are aggressive fighters they do not have any defense against predators or playful dogs without their horns. Dog-proof pens are almost essential, but they are also almost impossible without seriously hampering the activity level of the goats they contain.

Pygmies that are kept for pets, especially if they are to play with small children, would better be dehorned. Removing the horns from a small goat is relatively easy with an electric disbudding iron. Pygmy horns grow relatively slowly and can probably still be removed with ease up to the age of six weeks.

When the horns are just beginning to peak up through the hair, or earlier if preferred, the hair should be clipped from around the horn, close to the head. Then the preheated iron tip (hollow end) is placed over the horn button. The temperature should be tested on wood first. The wood should darken or blacken. The hot iron should not twist on the goat's head, but it should be rocked gently back and forth around the horn until the horn cap drops off. Then the exposed horn bud should burn

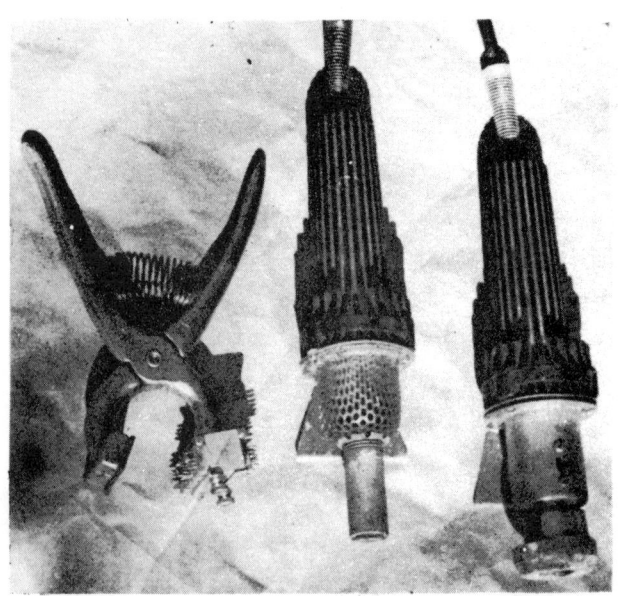

LEFT--LOADED 5/8" REVOLVING HEAD TATTOO PLIERS
CENTER--KID DEHORNING IRON: RIGHT CALF IRON
         FOR OLDER KIDS & DEODORIZING BUCKS

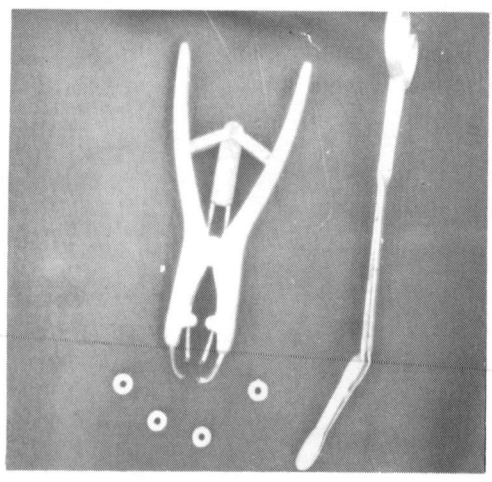

LEFT--ELASTRATOR & 4 DONUT BANDS FOR CASTRATING
RIGHT--GOOD FORCEPS FOR BOLUS & PILL DOSING

until it and the surrounding areas around the bud are copper colored. The iron should not be left on the head for more than fifteen seconds at a time. It should be removed and replaced and rocked until the job is done.

No dressing is needed over the burned area, but some people do use pine tar for fly control. The buds will drop off in about six weeks, leaving the head flat. If there is bleeding at the time the bud comes off, the wound should be treated with a topical ointment or other gentle dressing.

TATTOOING.

Tattooing is a highly recommended practice. In NPGA and AGS a tattoo is required for registration and for a show win to count and for the animals to be on production testing. Tattooing positively identifies each individual animal. It makes theft a little more difficult, and it makes falsification of registration papers more difficult. It is a good idea to demand a tattoo in an animal being purchased.

Tattooing is done with a pair of special pliers that holds letters made of metal needles. The tattoo is placed in the ear(s) by squeezing the pliers containing the desired letters into the inside of the ear. The ear and the letters should be cleaned first with alcohol.

After the punch is made, tattoo ink, (green works best in dark ears) should be rubbed into the holes. As the holes heal, the ink is trapped in them, and the tattoo should be legible for a long time--preferably the life of the animal.

Tattoo letters should be registered with the registry so that only one herd is using any given combination. There is no really standard practice for tattooing, but the one most frequently used is as follows:

Herd letters go in the right ear. Herd letters may be initials of breeder, first three letters of the herd name, or any other combination of three or four letters that is acceptable to the

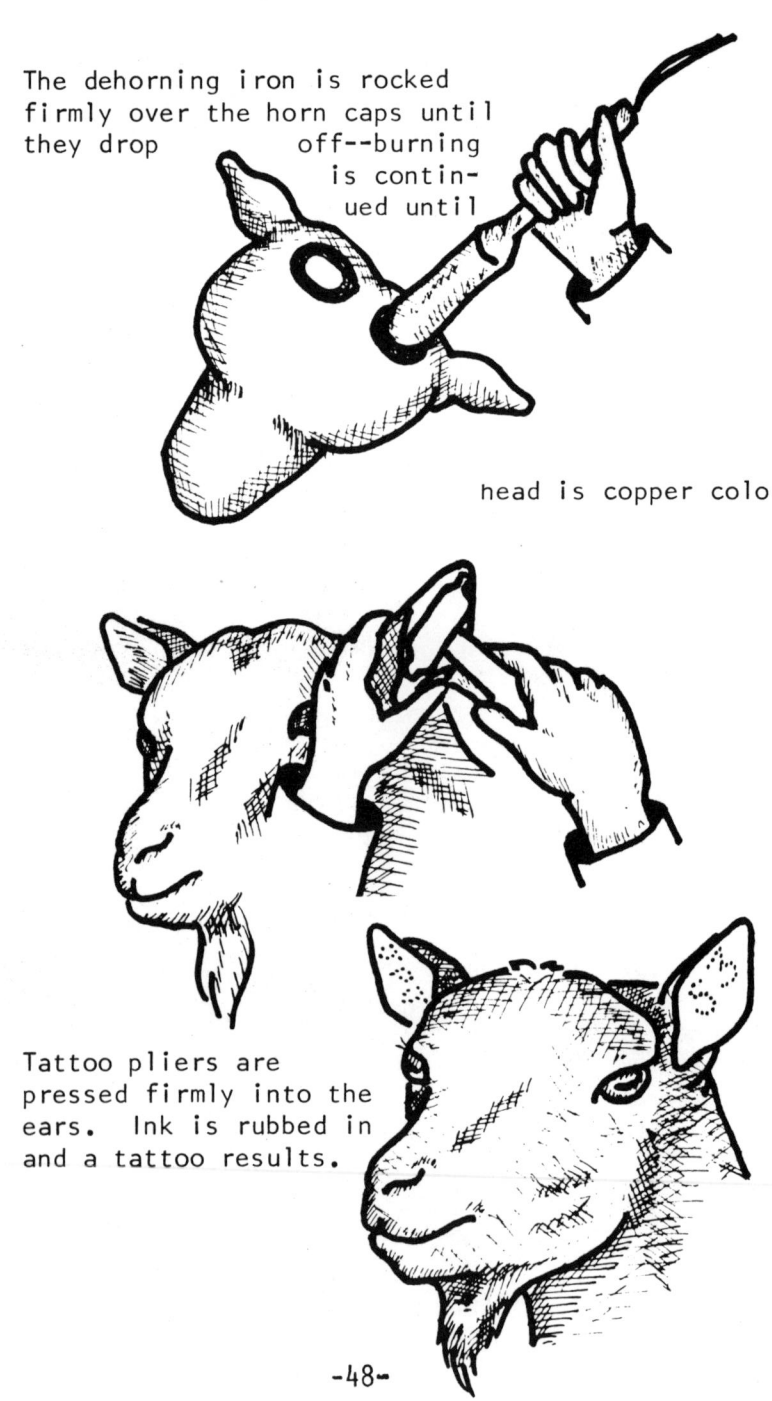

The dehorning iron is rocked firmly over the horn caps until they drop off--burning is continued until head is copper color.

Tattoo pliers are pressed firmly into the ears. Ink is rubbed in and a tattoo results.

breeder and the registry. This is the combination that should be confirmed by the registry.

Individual animal identification by year can go in the left ear. A letter is assigned to the year in which the kid is born. Sometimes the registry assigns a letter for a year. (S means 1982 for example,) but sometimes a breeder may select his own letter. The letter is followed by a number which indicates the chronological order in which the kid was born in that year.

Using that system, JPJ/S13 would be the thirteenth kid born to John Paul Jones in 1982.

But other systems may be used. Some breeders use the year itself instead of assigning a letter to it. The above kid, under that system, would be JPJ/ 1382.

If a breeder wishes to tattoo only one ear, the system can be condensed, and the above animal would be JJ132 or JJ213, all in one ear.

Because Pygmy ears are so small, quarter-inch letters and numbers are recommended, especially if the tattooing is done when the animals are kids. If the breeder waits until the animal grows up, a larger pair of pliers with the 3/8 inch letters can be used. However, if a breeder waits that long, he'd better be positive he can identify each animal with a certainty in the interim.

The herd identification number used in animals should be the one assigned to the breeder, or agreed upon by the breeder and the registry. It should be the letters assigned to the BREEDER. A breeder is always the owner of the dam at the time she is bred! The breeder's herdname, as well as his tattoo should be used on all kids, no matter who owns the doe at the time she kids.

WETHERING

All unneeded and undesirable bucks should be wethered or castrated so that they cannot contribute to the breed gene pool. Many Pygmies are castrated because the market for petstock is so big.

Most veterinarians in the past have been unwilling to recommend any method of castration except surgical. In the most common surgical method the bottom third of the scrotum is cut off with a sharp knife. The testicles are pulled one at a time through the bottom of the scrotum, and the cords attaching them are scraped until they are broken. Scraping, rather than cutting the cords, minimizes bleeding.

However, as more and more veterinarians are working with goats, more and more of them are beginning to recognize that the use of the elastrator is not as deadly as they had once assumed. It was not recommended much because of the chance of tetanus setting in when the scrotum started pulling away from the body. However, breeders much more often use the elastrator than surgery, and vets are seeing very few traumas and more good results than they had expected.

The elastrator is a pliers-like instrument with four prongs protruding on one face. A small rubber "donut" is put over the prongs, and when the pliers handles are squeezed together, the donut expands or opens. The scrotum and testicles of the small animal are pulled through the donut hole, and the handles are released slowly, leaving the donut around the top of the scrotum, separating the testicles from the body of the animal. In a matter of weeks, because circulation to the organs is cut off, they drop off, leaving a clean, smooth area. The final result is preferable in a cosmetic view to cutting. The elastrating best is done when the animal is very young. Older animals must be cut, or have the Burdizzo used. If that is done, the instrument must be used exactly according to instructions, or the operation will be incomplete.

For working around the rear of a Pygmy, the tail block can be used to keep it still. The tail is grasped firmly and pulled sharply up over the back to immobilize the rear quarters.

DEODORIZING

Some goat owners like to deodorize the bucks so neighbors don't complain, or whatever. Most of the buck's odor comes from musk glands located on his head. If a triangle is drawn from the cowlick to each horn, the musk glands are located on those lines just forward of the cowlick. They may be cut out, but there is an easier way if a buck is going to be dehorned.

Instead of dehorning a buck kid with the kid dehorning iron, if the calf dehorning iron is used it burns a large enough area to burn out the musk glands, too. In a larger buck kid, the odor can be detected when the gland is burned out.

Deodorizing is more pleasant for the owners, but some people who deodorize their bucks notice that it's harder to catch the does in heat. To deodorize bucks or not is a personal decision, but there are disadvantages in breeding. Since Pygmy bucks don't ever really go out of season as larger bucks do, a breeder might find it more aesthetically pleasing to deodorize.

Mid-1980's AGS Master Champion Morris's Bear, P-987, owned by Don Christensen, appeared to be a rare double-muscled buck who showed and threw excellent width, depth, angularity, and smoothness. His horns were straight, parallel, perhaps even crossed.

Well Goat---Sick Goat

Pygmies are a very healthy, hardy breed over all. Given proper management practices, a Pygmy owner can expect to have minimal problems with his animals. A healthy Pyqmy is a thing of joy and beauty. It is active, lively, somewhat aggressive and loving. Capricious (which comes from the root word for Caprine or goat) is a good description of the Pygmy.

A well Pygmy has a good appetite and bright full eyes. She is able to bounce when she walks or runs. She is gregarious and stays with, plays with the herd. If she's nursing, she's a conscientious mother. If she's pregnant, she gets very big and awkward, her attitude gentles down, but she remains her bright, alert, fairly active self. If she's milking, her production will be at least adequate for her kids, or enough better so the owner will want to take what's left. Her coat is smooth, and if it's short, it's glossy.

A healthy goat has a temperature range from $101°F$. to $104°F$--taken rectally. To take an accurate temperature, the rectum should be cleaned of fecal material that might interfere with work of the thermometer. The thermometer should always be cleaned before and after use with soap and water or alcohol. If the animal is very small, the end of the thermometer may be greased with Vaseline or K-Y Jelly. The average temperature is at $102.6°F$. A temperature over $104°F$ usually indicates infection, and a temperature under $101°F$ is indicative of toxicity. Antibiotics are usually used to fight infection, and electrolytes are good for supportive therapy in fighting toxins.

A healthy goat has a respiration rate of 15-20 breaths per minute. Respiration can be checked by holding a mirror in front of the nostrils. Each time the mirror fogs up, a breath has been taken (more specifically, exhaled.)

The normal pulse rate of the goat ranges from 64 to 80 beats per minute. The easiest place to take the pulse of the goat is on the carotid artery under the jaw of the animal. Firm pressure with two or three fingers will pick up the pulse very well. The thumb should NOT be used in counting pulse, as it has a light pulse of its own that could interfere.

The rumen of the healthy goat rotates about twice a minute. Sometimes it can be seen rolling just below the loin on the left side of the goat, and sometimes it can be felt by pressing the fist into the hollow on the left side. If the animal is chewing her cud, her rumen is working.

Normal blood pressure in a goat is about the same as in a human--120/80. It is difficult to take the blood pressure of a goat, but if blood vessels in the eye start breaking, the pressure is too high.

A healthy goat has bright pink membranes, especially inside the lower eyelids. A change to orange may indicate jaundice, and a drop to pale pink or white indicates anemia. A bluish eyelid could indicate lack of oxygen.

THE SICK GOAT

Many goat owners, even those who have owned them for decades, very often don't recognize sick goats. Granted, many "sicknesses" are self-limiting, and the animal recovers without any help, but it certainly behooves a conscientious goat owner to understand when a goat is sick.

Goats are individuals, and each animal will probably show its discomfort in a unique way. So an owner must know each animal. Knowing the individuals in a herd is the best way to recognize illness in a herd when it strikes.

Generally, any change in attitude, appetite, stance, gait, or production indicates the animal is not feeling well. If a goat with a good appetite suddenly starts getting picky, it's time to check other things. If a friendly goat becomes an isolate, or if an independent goat suddenly wants attention, the owner should check to find out why. If stance changes so that the head hangs low, or the topline sags or bows, or the rump is pulled even lower than Pygmy rumps are, or a leg is being favored, the owner better look for reasons. If the hair coat stands up on end, looks or feels dry, other things better be checked. If a goat limps, drags a leg, or drops behind the herd instead of bouncing along in her normal gait, there is a reason that needs to be found. If a milking doe who is not into pregnancy suddenly starts drying off, she's not well. If kids nursing a doe act hungry and dissatisfied, the owner better take a look at mama to see what might be wrong with her.

So the owner has noticed a change in attitude, appetite, stance, gait, or production--then what? The animal should be checked over as completely as possible. If the following questions are answered before a veterinarian is called, he will appreciate the information and know more what he should do:

What is the temperature?
Is she chewing her cud?
Is the milk normal, white and sweet, or is it curdled, lumpy, clotted, or bloody?
Is the neck straight and strong, or is it in a crooked or hanging position? Pygmies seem to have a propensity for neck injuries.
Are there any swellings or any inflammation?
Is she limping?
Is she on her feet? If not, is she lying in a normal position? Can she get up--with help or without help? If she's pregnant and very large, a doe sometimes gets on her back and is stuck as sheep sometimes get. This can kill an animal!
Is her coat rough? Is it dry?
Is she alert or uncaring?
Are there any abnormal discharges from any of

the body orifices? Abnormal discharges include blood, mucus, foam, pus, vomitus or cud, from the nose, mouth, anus, vagina (except that a doe that has kidded normally discharges from her vagina as long as two weeks), ears, eyes. Scours (diarrhea) is also an abnormal condition.
    Are the eyes sunken?(a sign of dehydration).
    Are the eyes dull?
    Are the membranes of the lower eye lids pale, orange, or bluish, or are they normal bright pink?
    Is she breathing regularly and clearly, or is her breathing rapid, shallow, rasping or otherwise abnormal?
    Is her pulse steady and regular, or does it seem thin and thready, racing, slow and irregular or in any other way abnormal?
    Is there any evidence of bloating--that is a swelling on the left side of the abdomen?
    If an owner can answer all these questions to himself and for a veterinarian, diagnosis is very close. Inexperienced owners should always call a veterinarian if an animal exhibits more than two or three abnormal symptoms. Experienced owners may have enough medications on hand they can muddle their way through, but for a really sick goat, a veterinarian should be called.
    It is important to establish a good working relationship with a veterinarian because part of his job is to help an owner keep his herd healthy. If a veterinarian is acquainted with the healthy herd, it will be easier for him to recognize and diagnose illness within that herd.
    Most Pygmies start out hardy and healthy. It is the job of the owner to keep them that way! A lot can be done to keep a goat herd healthy. The four main steps to keeping a healthy herd---sanitation, nutrition, isolation, and vaccination are discussed here.
    SANITATION means cleanliness--of barns, pens, feed, water, feeders, water troughs, bedding, the animals and their handlers. Sanitation is dis-

cussed elsewhere in this book.

NUTRITION--that is good nutrition, is essential to good health. Basic guidelines are found in this book, but no one really understands what entails good nutrition in a goat, so everyone makes a lot of mistakes.

ISOLATION is a sure way to keep healthy animals healthy. Isolation means keeping a healthy herd away from any animals that may not be in as good health. Strict isolation would mean no outside buck services, no showing, no moving for any reason, no loans or purchases. Many Pygmy owners do find this impractical for their purposes, so they must be prepared to combat exposure to disease by vaccination and treatment.

VACCINATION is essential for all herds that are on the move for any reason. Vaccination may even be needed in an isolated herd if particular disease problems exist in the area where it is.

Some common bacterins used on goats are the Bovibac I, and Lepto. Common bacterin-toxoid combinations are Tetanus, Clostridium perfringens, & some viral vaccines available are PI_3, OVA, BVD, IBR, and Blue Tongue.

A bacterin is a killed bacteria injection to cause an animal to build up resistance to the organism without exposing it to the live danger. A regular program of Pasturella bacterin use (found in Bovibac I) will help prevent shipping fever in a herd that is shown, shipped, sold or taken out for breeding.

Bovibac I by Fort Dodge combines Pasturella with Corynebacteria in this bacterin. This is a good idea because goats are very susceptible to abscesses caused, usually, by Corynebacteria. The University of Oregon (3) mentioned Corynebacteria abscesses as one of their major health problems in their Pygmy herd. Pygmies don't seem to show as many abscesses as the other breeds, but they are susceptible, and they should be vaccinated if exposure is expected. Just because no animals with abscesses are in a show doesn't mean they are not carrying Coryne. That organism can be harbored in the lungs and passed on the breath--even from animals that have no abscesses, as research at Michigan State University showed.

Most veterinarians recommend Tetanus Toxoid annually for goats. Goats are highly susceptible to "lock jaw" or tetanus, and use of this toxoid is not a bad idea. Regular use of the toxoid will protect animals from tetanus during such traumatic operations as dehorning, wethering, tattooing. If an owner is not sure whether or not his animals have had the Toxoid, an injection of Tetanus Antitoxin at the time of these operations is good management. Antitoxin will give fast, short-term protection, while the Toxoid gives slower, long-term protection.

Enterotoxemia or "overeating disease" (which is not necessarily caused by overeating), caused by the organism Clostridium perfringens types (B), C and D, can be devastating in a herd of goats. An annual injection of the Clostridium perfringens, types C & D bacterin gives some measure of protection against this disease unless stress is severe. Fuller protection against more of the Clostridial organisms can be gained by using a mixed bacterin-toxoid, like Electroid 7. However, care must be used not to overdose at all, as the medication is deadly if not used correctly.

Goats are highly susceptible to Leptospirosis, and use of the Lepto-5 bacterin is probably a good idea. It is not unheard of for goats to be carrying all five kinds of Lepto.

The viral diseases, like Parinfluenza (PI_3), Ovine Viral Abortion (OVA), Bovine Viral Diarrhea (BVD), Infectious Bovine Rhinotracheitis (IBR), & Blue Tongue can and do hit goats on occasion. But there is controversy about the use of live-viral vaccines, so most goat owners take their chances with the disease rather than vaccinate until it becomes absolutely necessary. Sometimes that is a good rule to follow on all bacterins & toxoids as well--don't use them until a need is shown. The protection is not absolute, anyway, but use of the medications mentioned here does help.

Stress triggers most diseases, so keeping the herd happy is a good way to keep it healthy. Some animals are more susceptible to stress than others and if a herdsman can select for stress-resistant animals, he will be ahead in the long run. Selection of this type of animal is discussed elsewhere in the book.

EQUIPMENT

Obviously, if a goat owner is going to vaccinate goats, he will have to have equipment on hand. The bacterins themselves must be ordered fresh for each usage, but other equipment can be kept handy.

NEEDLES--size 18 or 20 are best. Smaller diameter needles are available, but they are usually closely controlled and hard to obtain. Length of one-half inch is good for IM (intramuscular) shots and 1½ inch needles are good for IP (interperitoneal) and IV (intravenous) injections. Sub-Q (Subcutaneous) shots may need a 3/4 inch needle, and a quarter inch needle may be needed for ID (intradermal) shots. Most owners will not be doing any IV or ID work, and many will not even use IP.

SYRINGES--1cc, 3 cc, 12 cc, 35cc, & 60cc are the most frequently used syringes and best to keep on hand. Disposable syringes may be reused if they are soaked in a weak Nolvasan solution for 48 hours.

A THERMOMETER for taking rectal temperatures is absolutely essential, and a STETHOSCOPE for listening to hearts and lungs is nice, although not essential. The ear alone works fairly well.

INJECTIONS

Most bacterins are to be given Sub-Q. A good way to give Sub-Q injections is low on the rib cage where the skin is loose. Right behind the point of the elbow is a convenient location. The skin is pulled out away from the body to make a "V" shape with the base of the "V" against the ribs. Needle insertion into the "V" is done with the needle parallel with the body of the animal, and the medication is deposited in the hollow of the "V". The skin is released, and it lays back against the body over the medication. Sub-Q injections are absorbed slowly--sometimes taking as long as two days for the absorption to be complete. Bacterins given this way, especially the Clostridial bacterins, often leave a lump on the vaccination site.

Most other medications are given IM. One of the best sites for an IM injection is in the rump about half way between the hip bone and pin bone and about half way between the spine and thurl. It doesn't seem like there's enough muscle there for that purpose, but there is IF a short, $\frac{1}{2}$" or so, needle is used. If the rump is inconvenient because of animal movement, a good secondary site for IM injections is at the base of the neck in the muscle at the juncture with the shoulder. A short needle should be used to avoid hitting any bone or nerve. These two sites have fewer complications with blood vessels or nerves than any other site. Many goat owners have been told to give shots in the thigh. This will work for a while, but eventually an animal will go lame, & the owner will switch to a recommended site.

IV and IP injections are absorbed almost immediately and should be used when time is essential to keep an animal alive. However, both can be dangerous and should be learned before being used. IV involves the use of the jugular vein or the mammary veins. The jugular is best, and it is not difficult to find or hit, but it does require a second person to hold the head of a goat up and to one side to expose the site of a vein. Pressure low on the neck in the hollow beside the trachea causes the vein to bulge out for easy access. The needle should be inserted into the vein almost parallel with the vein to avoid going through the vein. For injections, the needle should probably point toward the heart, & the pressure below released before the injection is made. For drawing blood for culture, the needle should point away from the heart and the pressure on the vein held until the sample is taken.

IP injections go into the hollow below loin on RIGHT side of the goat's body. A long needle is used, and it is inserted toward the rear of the animal in the center of the hollow about an inch down from the boney ridge at the top.

Before any injection is given, aspiration is to be done. The plunger of the syringe should be pulled back before it is pushed in to release the medication. For IV, aspiration should show blood in the syringe. For all other injections, there should be no blood or other fluid seen in the syringe on aspiration. Blood shows if a vein's hit.

MEDICATIONS

Bacterins must be purchased and used fresh. Other medications can be kept on hand to use when they are needed. There are four kinds of medications that every goat owner should have on hand if he intends to do any of his goat treating himself. The four are antibiotics, antihistamine, epinephrine, and electrolytes.

ANTIBIOTICS are medications that will inhibit bacterial growth and activity, thus lessening the effects of the disease and allowing the animal to regain control and recover. Most bacteria are beneficial, so it's best not to use so many antibiotics that all bacteria are inhibited. However enough antibiotic should be used to bring harmful bacteria under control. Penicillin is the most frequently used antibiotic, and it is often more effective when it is paired with Streptomycin, in something like Combiotic. Such an antibiotic must be used for at least three days to be effective. A one-shot treatment usually does more harm than good. The long-acting penicillins like Bicillin that can be used every other day and are in the bloodstream for up to ten days are also popular. Erythromycin or Terramycin are good for the respiratory diseases, and Terramycin may be helpful in treating some of the arthritis problems, too.

EPINEPHRINE must be handy whenever any other medication is used--bacterin, antibiotic, or anything. Epinephrine is used to counteract adverse reactions an animal might have to other medications. Epinephrine must be given quickly to prevent death when an animal reacts badly, so it is best to carry it to the barn whenever any other medication is being given.

ANTIHISTAMINE should often be used with antibiotics to reduce swelling and inflammation give the animal comfort and help the antibiotic to work more effectively. Some veterinarians say,"If you are using antibiotics, you should be using antihistamines, too." Other vets prefer using steroids, but they can be dangerous with too much use. However, if a goat herd is in an area where snake bite is a danger, if antivenin cannot be kept on hand, steroids should be. Antihistamine will kill a snake-bit goat, but Cortisone just might help it pull through.

ELECTROLYTES have saved more "down" goats in many breeders' experience than any other medication. Electrolytes can be administered IV, IP, IM or Sub-Q, but if they are needed fast in an animal that is dying, they'd better go in IV or IP to go to work fast. Electrolytes help to balance the ions of the body, and if they are paired with the amino acids and B Vitamins, as they often are, a goat is helped back to good health. Calcium injections are often helpful with or instead of the electrolytes, but calcium is difficult to administer without causing flesh to slough off. Calcium has to be given IV and very slowly, and this is best done by a vet.

One form of antibiotics that should be kept on hand for milking animals, especially if they are not being milked, just nursed, is the udder infusion form. Mastitis is bound to hit a milking herd sooner or later, and it's best to be prepared to fight it. Probably the best way to fight a mastitis infection in a milking doe is to infuse the udder with something that contains penicillin and neomycin, and then give the doe injections of erythromycin. That combination may be reversed, but either way it usually manages to whip a case of mastitis unless it's a very difficult kind. If the doe is nursing kids, they should probably be pulled away so they don't suck out the medicine. Infusions should be given after each milking for at least two days. Injections should be given for at least three days.

    An udder is not difficult to infuse. The infusion syringe comes equipped with a long plastic tip, which can be inserted into the orifice of the teat. The tip is, presumably, sterile, & the end of the teat should be cleaned thoroughly with alcohol or iodine, or maybe even Nolvasan so that no bacteria are forced into the udder along with the infusion. The entire contents of the syringe should be used during an infusion. Just because the udder is smaller doesn't mean part of the medication should be held back for next time. Besides, that's unsanitary! After the medication has been pushed into the udder by the plunger in the syringe, the syringe is withdrawn, and the medication should be massaged into the udder.

    IODINE has been mentioned several times, and it is important for a goat owner to have 7% (vet strength) iodine on hand. It should be stored & used in such a way that it will not become contaminated and lose its effectiveness. Iodine is not a sterilant or a disinfectant, but it is a good cleansing agent. It is very effective when combatting the micro-organisms that cause abscesses, and this is one of its primary uses, along with dipping navels of newborns.

    If a goat owner has problems with abscesses, it is best to let the abscess "ripen." When it is "ripe," it will start to lose its hair and be soft in the middle. It is not a good idea to let the abscess (boil) break on its own, because the exudate is spread over everything the animal may touch, and the disease spreads more readily to other animals. It is best to lance the ripe boil by incising it with a razor blade--low on the boil so it drains well. All the exudate, which will be a creamy or cheesy pus, should be squeezed into a paper and burned. If the boil is open wide enough the inside should be scraped with cotton swabs, paper toweling or some other disposable material to be burned with the rest of the exudate.

When the boil is as clean as it can be, it is to be rinsed out with clear water by using an ear syringe with a flexible bulb, and then finally it should be rinsed with 7% iodine, also through the syringe. If it is a very deep boil, it may have to be packed with gauze soaked in 7% iodine. Use of topical antibiotics will not be effective with iodine, but injectible antibiotics won't hurt any.

An animal may be completely free of external abscesses, and die of internal abscesses. An animal may also be completely free of all abscesses, and still be harboring the organisms in the lungs or tonsil area to spread to other goats on its breath. Unbroken external abscesses are not deadly or even dangerous, but they are annoying.

THE RUMP AND SHOULDER--PRIMARY AND SECONDARY I.M. INJECTION SITES

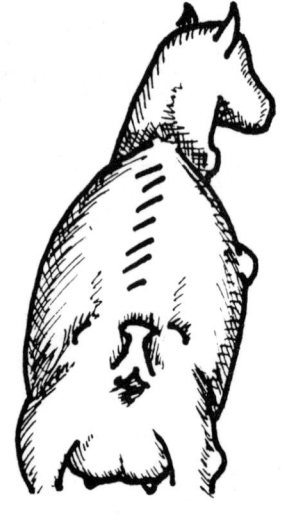

LEFT: MAIN LOCATIONS OF THE COMMON ABSCESSES

RIGHT TOP: A TYPICAL-LOOKING ABSCESS

RIGHT BELOW: AN ABSCESS THAT HAS BEEN PROPERLY LANCED AND DRAINED AND RINSED

Breeding & Kidding

If a breeder wants his herd to improve, if he wants the breed in general to improve, he will be careful in selecting sires for his does. He should study pedigrees, show records, classification numbers and production records and select bucks that will complement his herd and improve it in the direction he wants to go.

If a breeder considers his does to be leggier than he'd like, he would be wise to use a buck with very short cannon bones. If his does tend to be a little taller than he'd like, he'd better select a buck with short stature. If his does are too refined to suit him, use of a heavy buck should help. If his does are too narrow for his tastes, he must use a wide buck. If he needs better udders on his does, he should use a buck whose dam and daughters have good udders. If he's aiming for milk production, he should again look at the dam and daughters and sisters of a buck.

As artificial insemination becomes more popular and effective in Pygmies, a wider selection of bucks will be available to all breeders. The more records available for bucks in the AI program, the better. It takes years to "prove" a buck, so only those with records should be used widely in AI.

If a breeder is satisfied with the width, proportions and height of his does, he should still be careful in selecting a buck that shows the same desirable proportions so the kids will not be less than their dams.

Selecting a buck to use on a herd is a chore that should take considerable time, thought and research. Selecting a buck from a herd whose owner can be trusted to be objective and honest will also help. If temperament is important to an owner, he should take the time to meet the buck he plans to use. A friendly, docile buck out of a friendly and docile mother will probably throw friendly & docile kids. A mean buck or a flighty buck should certainly not be used on does that exhibit those same tendencies if the owner wants kids he can be close to and work with.

Before artificial insemination becomes widely used in Pygmies, a good evaluation system should be established, making use of production records, classification scores, show records and including special information on such things as temperament, special strengths, life spans, and weaknesses.

University of Oregon (3) found the Pygmy to be a seasonal breeder, breeding once a year from August to March. However, although the conception rate may be a bit lower other times of the year, most Pygmy owners are finding that Pygmies will breed any time of year and even kid twice a year. They are also finding, however, that a doe which kids frequently may have fewer kids per conception and that she may become run down and need a rest period after a few kiddings. If the buck runs in with the rest of the herd, the breeder will be more likely to get the second kidding each year than if the buck is housed separately & the does are "hand bred."

The doe carries her kids for five months, and a milking doe should be dried off to have six to eight weeks rest before she kids again. If milk is being used for human consumption, the odor of the buck may permeate it, making it less than desirable. If so, the owner may wish to separate his bucks from his does for that reason. If more than one buck is being used on a herd of does, it is obvious the bucks will have to be housed separately and the does hand bred.

All breeds of goats mature quickly. A buck is almost always fertile by the time he is eight or ten weeks old, so all bucks should be wethered or separated from the herd at that time if a goal of controlled breeding is to be met. Does, too, may mature as early as three months, but they should not actually be bred much before they are half a year old, and that's still pretty early. A doe that kids at eight or nine months could have a very hard time, especially if she is carrying a large single kid. Besides that, an immature dam sometimes takes a lot of encouragement before she is willing to care for her kids. Pygmies usually are excellent mothers, however, and need very little help in raising their young.

There are many different kinds of breeding plans that can be used very successfully.

CROSSBREEDING is usually done accidentally. It involves breeding a doe of one breed to a buck of a different breed. For example, if a Pygmy buck breaks through his fence and breeds a Nubian doe, the result is now called Kinder. The earless Pygmy-LaMancha crosses are quite popular in some areas, and some people purposely cross a Pygmy with their larger breeds to get smaller does for easier handling without much drop in the production. Crossbreeding puts a lot of "hybrid vigor" into the kids, but it seldom serves much useful purpose. Especially when a Pygmy is involved, the size and productivity of the crossbred offspring would almost certainly be less desirable than either parent. So crossbreeding is not recommended.

OUTCROSSING involves breeding a sire of one line of Pygmies with a doe from a different line within the same breed. Such breedings, especially from inbred lines, are very acceptable, giving the kids a measure of "hybrid vigor" without losing breed type.

LINEBREEDING takes place when both buck and doe are from the same family "line." They would both be the same type and from the same family, but the breeding would not be really close. Linebreeding would involve breeding animals distantly related to one common ancestor.

INBREEDING is the closest kind of breeding

that can be done, and a breeder can be very successful using it, IF he selects carefully so he does not breed together animals with like weaknesses. Inbreeding involves half-brother-half-sister matings, sire-daughter combinations or a breeding of dam and son, or sometimes even full siblings. Obviously, because the genetic makeup is so similar between these animals, care must be used in selecting breeding partners. Weakness of ANY kind seen in both parents will be intensified in the kids, so animals with like weaknesses must not be used for inbreeding (or, for that matter, any other kind of breeding). Likewise, though, similar strengths will also be intensified in the kids, so that is when a program of inbreeding becomes successful.

    A frequently successful plan in breeding is to outcross in one breeding to try for the kind of animal a breeder wants, and then, if he finds it in the kids, inbreed the kids. Kids from such outcrosses can usually be bred to full siblings without any genetic hangups. How close a breeder wants to take a chance going after that first inbreeding is up to him.

KIDDING

    One disadvantage of pen-breeding is to not have accurate dates for kidding of the does. Although a doe can kid quite successfully with the herd out in the pasture, it would probably be a lot more ideal if she were penned alone in an area that had clean bedding. It's best if a kidding stall has been cleaned and sanitized before the clean, fresh bedding is put down.

    Probably 95% of all Pygmy does have their kids without any assistance or any need of any, but on occasion some help is necessary. If a breeder must help a doe to kid, he should observe all methods of cleanliness. His hands should be thoroughly washed up to the elbow. The vulva of the doe should be washed. If forceps or chains or other delivery devices are used, they should be sterilized.

If the owner is with the doe at time of kidding and it is a normal, unassisted delivery, the owner should 1) clean the nose and mouth of each kid, 2) dip the navels in 7% iodine (pour a little in a small container for each kid and throw away what is left after each dipping so the entire bottle is not contaminated), 3) make sure the teats of the doe are open, clean and functional, 4) watch for the afterbirth and remove it from the kidding area and bury it, 5) offer the doe some warm water to drink (which may be sweetened with honey or molasses) to replace the body heat and energy she has lost in her efforts, 6) make sure the kid sucks as soon as possible, but for sure within the first 30 minutes, to get the valuable protection he needs from the colostrum (first milk of the doe),7)watch to see that the kid passes the thick, black meconium (first bowel movement). If the meconium has not been passed within several hours, the kid may need an enema. When doe and kids are removed from the kidding pen, the bedding should also be taken away, and the area should be cleaned and sanitized for the next use.

KIDDING PROBLEMS

Most Pygmy does present their kids normally & kid easily. Normal presentation is nose first with it resting on both front legs. A secondary normal presentation is hind feet first. Either presentation will allow for a fairly easy delivery. If the presentation is normal, but the kid won't come all the way out, it is probably because he is too big and needs to be pulled. If an owner has to pull, the pulling should be done downward toward the hocks of the doe so that the kid follows the natural contour of the birth canal. If the kid doesn't pull easily, it should not be forced, as sometimes a kid's stifle joint hangs up on the doe's pelvis,

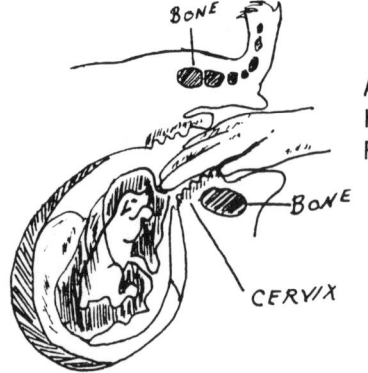

A NORMAL DELIVERY IS HEAD RESTING ON BOTH FRONT FEET

A ONE-LEG ONLY DELIVERY MAY POSSIBLY BE PULLED AS IS, BUT THAT IS NOT RECOMMENDED

REACHING IN WITH ONE HAND AND PULLING THE MISSING FOOT FORWARD BEFORE DELIVERY IS BETTER

and a hand will have to be sent in to release the hang-up before the kid will come.

If the kid won't come and only one leg is in view, the owner should slip an index finger along the neck of the kid, along the shoulder, hook his finger behind the bent knee of the kid's front leg and pull the leg into position. Then normal delivery and pulling is possible. However, it is often possible to pull a kid when only one front leg is visible.

Pygmies seem to have a propensity for having kids presented up-side-down. If a doe is in hard labor (and does should not be allowed to endure a hard labor for more than 20 minutes before something is done), and no kid is forthcoming, an owner should check things out. If the sack is broken, the position of the kid will be easier to ascertain, but then the delivery will have to be done as soon as possible. If the owner can feel teeth on the top side instead of the bottom side of the jaw, the presentation is up-side-down, and the kid will have to be turned into the normal position for delivery. The kid will have to be pushed into the uterus (should be done between the contractions of the doe). Then the owner should hold in place the head of the kid and turn the doe around it. If the doe is on her right side, rotate her around the kid and the owner's arm by rolling her on her back and to her left side. This is also not an easy task, but it is an essential one. Only if the kid is turned can it be pulled.

Transverse deliveries are also difficult. If the spine or ribs of the kid are presented with a head and feet pointing into the doe, again a kid will have to be pushed back into the uterus, rotated (the kid this time, not the doe), & pulled.

Breech, or tail presentations can also give problems. If the owner feels a tail when he goes in, he'll have to run his forefingers along rump or thigh until he can hook a hind leg around the hock and pull the leg into position for a hind-feet-first delivery. Again, pulling should be done in a downward direction.

Another problem Pygmies often have is for the head of the kid to be turned backward instead of resting on the front legs. The head is often hard to pull into position--harder than the legs are, but if the same kind of procedure is used, it can be done. Sometimes the kid has to be pushed slightly back into the uterus at the same time the head is being pulled into position. Keeping the head where it belongs is the problem in this kind of delivery.

Gentleness is essential in any kind of help a doe is given. The uterus will rupture and tear if the delivery is rough. Small hands work better in a doe than large hands, even if they lack strength of larger hands.

Probably any doe that has had manual help in kidding should have an antibiotic injection just to be on the safe side. A long-acting penicillin is good in such a case.

AGS MCH Pygmy Palace Molly, P-3657, was bred and owned by Sue McCullough.

Red/tan Pygmy Palace Dusty Rose, bred by Sue McCullough, shows that even champions climb wood piles.

Selecting

It's been written that Pygmies, or Lilliputs, as they are known in England, were on exhibition in that country at the Crystal Palace Show in 1875.

Pygmies have been on display at various fairs and shows for many years in this country, too. The Hearst Pygmies were displayed in a Northern California Show as early as 1967, and such notable big goat breeders as Bruce Schumacher and Ron Maahs often displayed Pygmies with their other breeds at a lot of fairs on the main circuit in California.

The first official, sanctioned Pygmy show in the United States was held at the Orange County Fall Fair in November, 1977. It was co-judged by Dr. Ralph Bogart and Alice Hall, and the champion doe of that show, Fort Werts Meg, bred and owned by Ann Werts, won her first championship there. She later went on to become the first doe eligible to be a Master Champion in American Goat Society.

SELECTING

Whether a person is a first-time Pygmy owner looking for animals to buy, an established Pygmy owner looking for a buck to breed to, or an established Pygmy breeder trying to decide which kids to keep or which animals to show, selecting a good Pygmy is of prime importance. Every showman must first be a judge, because selecting and judging should be done on the same principles.

The main difference is that the breeder or exhibitor compares the animal he sees with his ideal, and the judge compares the animal he sees with the other animals in the ring at the same time.

For better communication, every judge and exhibitor should know the parts of the Pygmy.

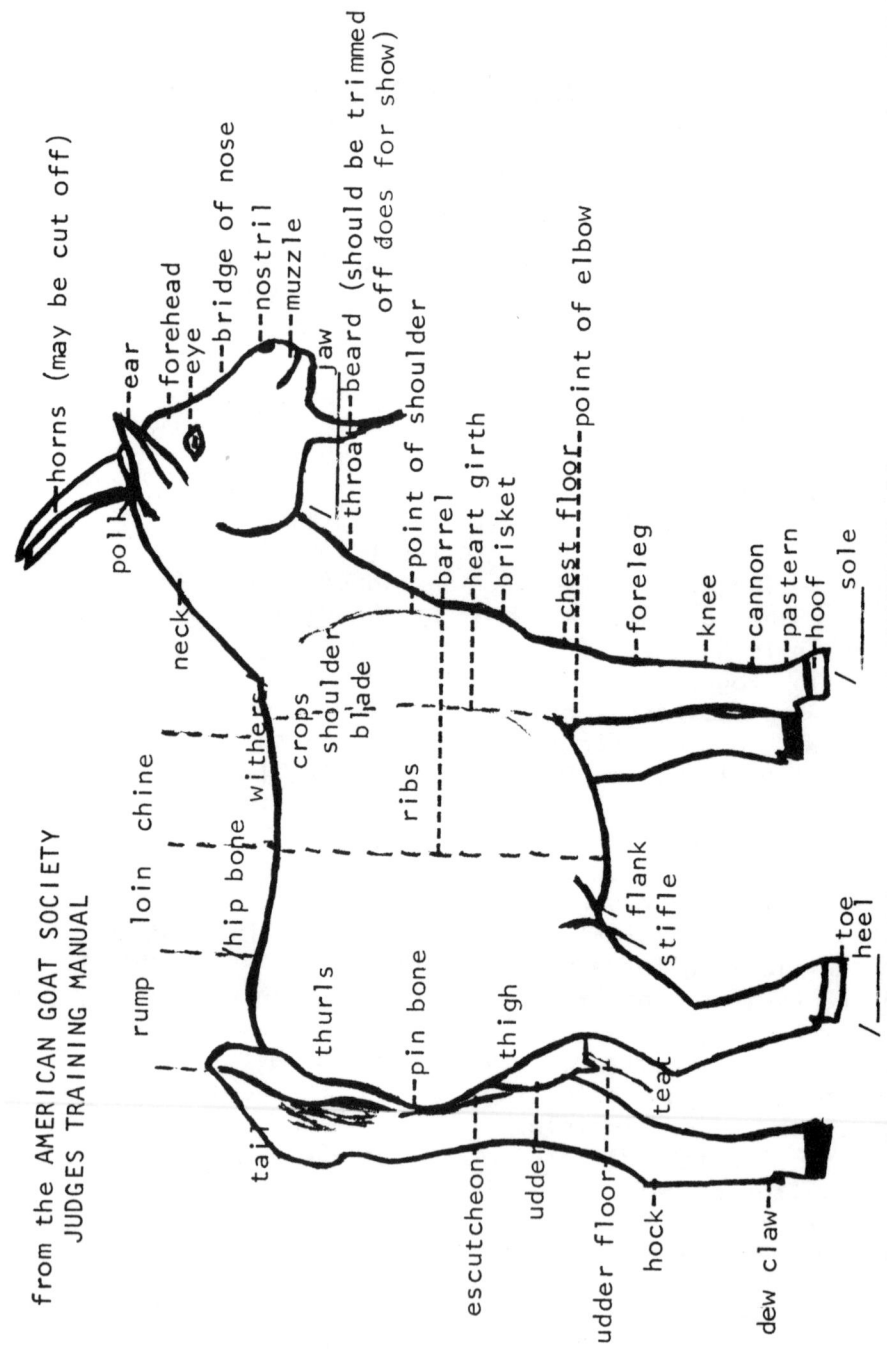

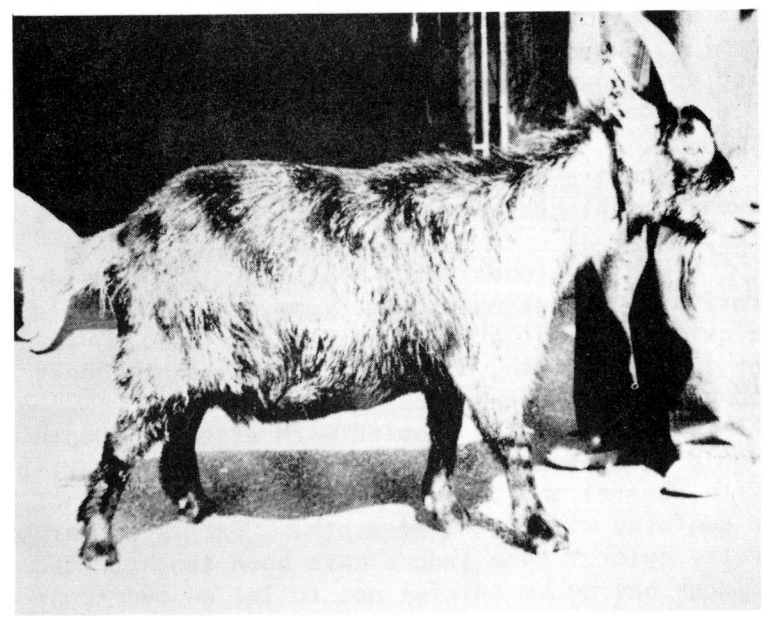

FORT WERTS MEG WON THE NATION'S FIRST OFFICIAL SHOW FOR PYGMIES, ORANGE COUNTY, CALIFORNIA, NOVEMBER, 1977. MEG LATER WENT ON TO QUALIFY AS THE NATION'S FIRST MASTER CHAMPION.

She has a very level topline & a fairly long and level rump for a Pygmy. She's alert and quite angular. This excellent doe was bred and owned by Ann Werts.

ANOTHER EXCELLENT DOE, RIGHT, IS NORSHAAM SILVER, A DOE BRED AND OWNED BY RON MAAHS. Silver was not yet registered at the first Pygmy Show, but she won Champion unregistered doe and Reserve Best in Show under Meg. She became a very angular doe with age and has prominent kids in both AGS and NPGA.

It's always easier and surer to select a mature animal. Kids are cute and bouncy and heartwarming, but it is not easy to select a kid and wind up with a winner. Selecting a mature animal if done correctly, can certainly lead to showing a winner.

There are some generalities about selecting, however, that can be shared with mature animals & kids.

WIDTH is probably the most important consideration in selecting a good Pygmy. Width should be evident in the muzzle, between the eyes, in the chest, heart girth, barrel, between the hip bones and pin bones, and between the legs.

DEPTH should be coupled with width. Depth should be apparent in the muzzle, chest, heartgirth, barrel and flank. "Beefiness" should not be confused with width or depth. "Fat is a very pretty color," some judges have been taught, and a judge has to be careful not to let an over-conditioned animal catch his eye. Fat can hide lots of other faults.

SUBSTANCE should be coupled with both width and depth. Substance is partly width and depth, but it is more than that. Heavy bone is also part of substance. Heavier boned animals usually have a stronger constitution than lighter boned animals. They resist stress better and tend to live longer. Given a choice between similar animals, the one with the heavier bone will probably have more strength and soundness.

SMOOTHNESS OF BLENDING is important in any animal because smoothly articulating joints also indicate soundness. Smoothness of blending can be best seen while the animal walks. The topline is to be fairly straight and stay that way while the animal moves. The rump should not be too steep either between the thurls or between the hips and pins, and its angle shouldn't change much as the animal moves. The head should be carried as high as a short, thick, little Pygmy neck can carry it, and the legs should be short, stocky, straight &

strong. Weaknesses in the shoulders, withers, topline and legs, especially the pasterns, may be best seen when the animal is walking.

BALANCE refers to proportions, but it's more than that, too. An animal is in balance when it has all its parts in correlation. No part of an animal should seem over-sized or under-sized in comparison with the rest of that animal, and the parts should hang together well. Balance is a combination of good proportions and smoothness of blending.

SELECTING A KID

If the animal being selected is not a milker the above description will cover most things. A kid should have plenty of width and depth. Yearling Pygmies tend to shallow out and not look as much like a Pygmy for a while. They will return to their Pygmy appearance as they get older. The width between hind legs is especially important. Pygmies have a tendency to "hock in" or have the hocks point toward each other. A Pygmy kid with straight hind legs when viewed from the rear is preferred to one that "hocks in." The arch in the escutcheon should be wide and full, not with a pointed, narrow top. The rump should be wider at the pin bones than at the hips, or at least look square.

From the front, the kid should have a short wide head with a very distinctive concave nose, or dish in the face. The eyes should be bright and clear, and the ears should be very short and alert. The front legs should be wide apart, and the chest floor should be very wide. The front legs should be short, heavy, and straight.

The reproductive organs and teats should be definitely checked when a kid is being purchased or selected for show. There should be only two teats, and they should be widely spaced apart & symmetrical. Each should have just one orifice, which, in older kids, can be felt by rubbing the teat between the thumb and forefinger. Having an orifice that can be felt is an indication that a

A GOOD PYGMY IS DEEP AND WIDE AND ANGULAR AND MUSCULAR AND HAS STRAIGHT, STRONG, WIDELY SPACED AND HEAVY LEGS. SHE HAS A ROUNDED, STRONGLY ATTACHED UDDER.

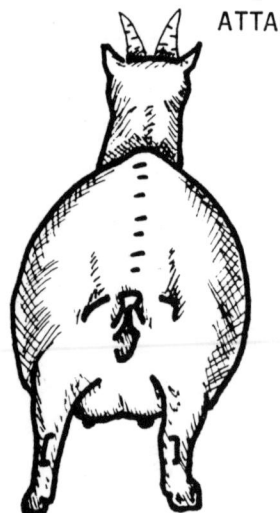

A POOR PYGMY IS JUST THE OPPOSITE, ALTHOUGH FEW ARE THIS POOR. IN GIVING REASONS THE JUDGE WOULD SIMPLY SAY THAT ONE (ON THE LEFT) IS WIDER, DEEPER, AND STRONGER IN THE TOPLINE AND LEGS THAN THE TWO DOE (ON THE RIGHT). HE MIGHT ADD THAT ONE ALSO HAS MORE ANGULARITY, A MORE WIDELY ATTACHED UDDER, MORE SUBSTANCE AND MORE STRENGTH.

doeling is mature enough to be bred. This sign is a better indicator of breeding age than either age or size. Partial udder development or uneven udder development on a dry doe that has not been bred is not discriminated against, as udders of that type usually balance out at kidding time.

The vulva should look normal size in comparison with the size of the doe, with no evidence of any rudimentary male organs, either in the vagina, or in the udder.

In checking buck kids, there should be only two teats, each with just one orifice. They should be evenly spaced on either side of the scrotum. The scrotum should contain two testicles at any age. A buck born with only one testicle or none at all is not likely to gain them with age. The scrotum is to be rounded and well attached. The testicles in a buck of any age should be firm and fill the scrotum.

The feet of the animal should be fairly square (heel same depth as toe), and not too splayed (with the toes spread apart.) Pygmies have a tendency to splayed feet because of the climbing they do in their natural habitat, but it is not a particularly desirable characteristic.

SELECTING A MILKER

Because 12-26 points on the score cards are used to define the udder, it is more accurate for a person to select a milker than a kid. Also, some items on the score card refer to a hard-to-define condition called "dairy character" which is often much more apparent in milkers than in dry stock.

After width, depth, substance, strength, legs and soundness, smoothness of blending, head and alertness have been evaluated, angularity deserves consideration. All mature Pygmy does should look angular. From the front, angularity will show in a triangle that has its point over the withers and widens into the chest and shoulders. This look will reveal width in the chest without fat carried over the withers. From the side, angularity will show with the apex of the triangle somewhere out in front of the doe, one line of the triangle following her topline, and the other being her underline. From the rear, two angles can be seen. One has the apex at the withers and widens out over the barrel(showing width of barrel), and the other has the apex at the withers and widens out over the hips, showing width between the hip bones. A third angle can be seen from the rear, with the apex at the vulva, and widening out into the hocks. All these angles are important. The wider the angles the better.

Hands should be used to determine soundness of an animal and udder quality. Soundness is felt in the joints while they are moving. There is to be no swelling, heat, grating or cracking. These things all indicate an animal is unsound. Feeling the udder shows both area of udder attachment, and texture.

To determine udder attachment, both hands are put around the top of the udder when it's full of milk, one hand from the rear, the other from the front, and the fingers of the hands shouldn't meet in an udder with excellent area of attachment. If the udder is empty, reaching to the fore udder from the rear and pulling back gently will reveal any front "pockets" in udder attachment. Visual confirmation with full udders helps. While a doe stands, hands are placed on her hips. Her udder should not sway much when she is rocked from side to side.

The texture of the udder is also important to dairy character. The udder should be soft, pliable and collapsible. There should be no lumps or scar tissue, no meaty feel or lumpy fatty tissue. Teats should be small enough to be in proportion to the size of the doe and the udder, but not too small to milk. If the doe is in milk, drawing a little milk from the udder will give an idea if a doe is the kind wanted in a milking herd. A hard milker or a doe with abnormal milk or small or large orifices is not a good buy. Abnormal milk probably indicates mastitis, which is usually hard to treat, and large orifices leave a doe more vulnerable to mastitis attacks. Small orifices make a doe hard to milk, and that is never fun.

Some other aspects of dairy character and good condition are the ribs, skin and hair. Pygmy ribs will feel rounded, but they should point toward the rear of the animal and have quite a bit of space between them. The skin over the ribs should be of soft texture and be pliable enough to pull away from the body easily. The hair should feel soft & silky and smooth.

SELECTING THE BUCK

Selecting a buck is more important & perhaps less accurate than selecting a doe. The buck is more important because if he is used on all does in a herd, he soon becomes 50% or more of the herd in the kids. Selecting a buck is perhaps less accurate because bucks usually show less angularity than does, they seldom show any milking potential (& if they do give milk, they possibly have a hormone imbalance that could interfere with fertility), and it takes years, almost the lifetime of the buck, to prove whether or not he did what he was hoped to do.

Everything that has been said about selecting kids and does (except the udder) goes double for a buck. Width, depth, alertness, soundness, smoothness are all more important in the buck than in the doe. Strong legs that are straight and show substance and are on strong pasterns and square hoofs are much more important in a buck. A buck with any weakness in the legs and feet cannot breed well.

The main difference comes in the bucks' masculinity and lack of angularity. Pygmy bucks seldom get the very wide and deep barrels the does do but their necks should be heavier and look shorter than the necks of the does. The buck will have a lot more hair growth on the neck and head, and the beard of the buck will be heavier, longer & coarser than the beards of the does. But no massive, handsome beard can make up for lacks in width or depth.

CAMEROON CRUSADE TAURUS, BRED BY RACHEL SAGASAR, AND OWNED BY DON AND AUDREE ANDERSON, WAS THE NATION'S FIRST MASTER CHAMPION BUCK.

His length of leg is excellent, & his muscling is fantastic. He was dehorned. A little more dish in the face would be more ideal, but Taurus is a very ideal buck. Bucks seldom look as angular or deep and wide in the barrel as the does.

Cameroon Crusade originated partly with the stock at Fresno State University, California, as Rachel Sagasar was the herdsman there. Dr. Art Hoversland, who had also worked with Corinne Odiorne, was in charge.

If a buck is clipped for show, his beard & mane should remain intact to show masculinity!

Taurus was bred to yearling Critter Country Bonnie, who had quadruplets for her first freshening. Her second kidding, a year later, yielded quintuplets, which was quite a record for a doe--nine kids in her first two kiddings. But Bonnie wasn't through yet. In her third kidding she produced seven kids, for a total of 16 kids in three litters. That's quite a record! All the kids lived but the last one--he wasn't expected!

Score Cards

It is easy to tell from comparing score cards what each registry emphasizes and why it is difficult to have dual-sanctioned shows. All the cards are based on a total of 100 points.

	AGS Does	AGS Bucks	IDGR Does	IDGR Bucks	NPGA Does	NPGA Bucks
Appear.	14	20	10	10	14	14
Head	8	10	6	5	10	12
Horns	0	0	4	6	0	0
Coat	0	0	0	5	4	6
Markings	0	0	0	0	8	12
Neck	3	5	3	4	3	5
Shoulder	5	8	10	10	5	5
Chest	10	13	7	10	10	10
Barrel	10	10	8	10	8	8
Skin/Ribs	4	7	10	11	0	0
Flank	0	0	2	4	0	0
Back	inc. above		5	5	8	8
Rump	10	10	5	5	8	8
Ft./Legs	10	17	10	12	10	12
Mammary	26	0	20	0	12	0
Testicles	0	0	0	3	0	0

(AGS and NPGA figure testicles are either correct or disqualified.)

Because of NPGA's emphasis on the Pygmy as a pet, it has developed a score card for judging the wethers: General appearance=12; head & breed markings= 8 each; neck, shoulders, forelegs, hindlegs = 5 each; chest, barrel, back, rump=6 each; feet &

coat = 4 each; general health and showmanship are given 10 each, for a total of 100. AGS judges for years have been asked to judge wethers in all the breeds, but they have never used a separate score card. They have been judging wethers as meat animals, and they basically use the buck score card by modifying it to give less emphasis on legs & feet and more emphasis on muscular (not masculine) conformation.

EVALUATING FAULTS

There is no perfect Pygmy. Every Pygmy has a fault or two. Just how serious these faults are is spelled out in the faulting sheet. Disqualifications should be avoided in all breeding and show animals. Animals with disqualifications are choice for the meat market.

Disqualifications include hornlessness, " roman" or arched nose, pendulous ears, uncharacteristic proportions (legs too long, body too narrow,)*
*except that NPGA defines this as being not cobby, and makes it only a serious fault), and being oversized (too tall at the withers) or too long in the cannon bone. Every judge and every breeder should have a way to evaluate these two things without a yard stick and calipers. Using the palm of a hand or the length of a leg in a given pair of shoes is often a help.

Other disqualifications are serious emaciation (seldom seen in a Pygmy), total blindness, permanent lameness, (judges should be cautious about calling some of these things), non-functioning half of udder or non-function teat, extra teats (including bifurcal or spur teats) that interfere with milking or that are functional, extra teats on bucks, abnormal milk (not in NPGA), crooked face (on bucks only in AGS), evidence of hermaphroditism or any other inability to reproduce, one testicle on buck or none at all, permanent physical defects (such as navel hernias). NPGA also has as a disqualification the lack of all breed-specific markings, which is another reason dual-shows are difficult. AGS has no problem with solid-colored animals of the Pygmy breed.

Very serious faults in AGS only are an udder lacking in size in comparison with the doe (not often seen in Pygmies), extra teat on a doe (even if it has been cut off), double orifice in teat, crooked or malformed feet (including very flat feet or shallow heels (not usually seen on Pygmies and only moderate fault in NPGA), and crooked face on does (disqualification in NPGA). NPGA drops a double orifice to serious and adds in very serious poor health, eyes too close, undershot or over or parrot jaw , thin or weak neck and curly or long hair coat.

Serious faults are pendulous udders, udders too distended to feel texture, udders hard or swollen except in does just fresh. NPGA adds poor condition, protruding eyes, slight over or under shot jaws in adults, wavy or silky coat, some of the breed specific markings being absent or indistinct, and optional or unusual markings.

Moderate to serious faults depending on the degree are loose, winged or heavy shoulders; narrow chest; pinched heart girth; shallow or narrow body; low or sway backed; steep rump; long rump; small boned for existing body size; bowed legs in front; buck knees; shallow or weak thighs; legs too long; hind legs close; pasterns sprung -- all of which are just moderate in NPGA. AGS adds the teats not being clearly delineated from the udder.

Slight to moderate faults depending on degree are less than excellent udder attachments (this is just moderate in NPGA), lacking separation between halves of udder (common in Pygmies), too much separation between halves of udder, beefy udder, major pocket in fore udder, scar tissue in udder, close in hocks, undershot or overshot jaws (these are more serious in NPGA).

Moderate faults are large horn scurs or stubs on dehorned Pygmies, nondisabling lameness, knees that are enlarged, feet turned out or crooked, a Pygmy that is undersized, or one with a snipy muzzle or thin or weak neck (very serious in NPGA), or a Pygmy with small or round eyes or protruding eyes (serious in NPGA), teats that are too close, bulbous, large, small, uneven, pointed sideways, hard to milk or with small streams or leaking. NPGA adds poorly groomed, coat too short or sparse.

The only slight fault in AGS is a wry or broken tail that might interfere with kidding.

The short, stocky Pygmy neck seems to be a weak spot in the breed. They are easily broken & dislocated, so any crooks in necks should be avoided when animals are being selected.

Now, how is this list of faults used in judging? The usual procedure is to consider a serious fault serious only up to the number of points allocated for that part of the body. If head has ten points, large scurs or horn stubs can only be detracted up to ten points (except that it's unlikely the full allotment of points could ever be subtracted if that part of the body is there at all.) More points can be taken if the fault also affects general appearance. Undelineated teats can only affect an animal up to five points, unless they detract from general appearance, too. Points don't apply to disqualifications. Disqualifications in any minor point take the animal out of competition!

FITTING FOR SHOW

If a Pygmy has good all-around care, with good nutrition, sanitation, vaccination, hoof trimming, tattooing, clipping, very little may need be done to ready her for a show. Hoofs should be trimmed just before a show so the animal will walk better. There is considerable controversy about whether a Pygmy should be clipped for show, but this is part of the growing pains of the breed. In the early days of the first goat shows of other breeds, many exhibitors thought it was "cheating" to clip their animals. Hair coat is an indicator of purity of a

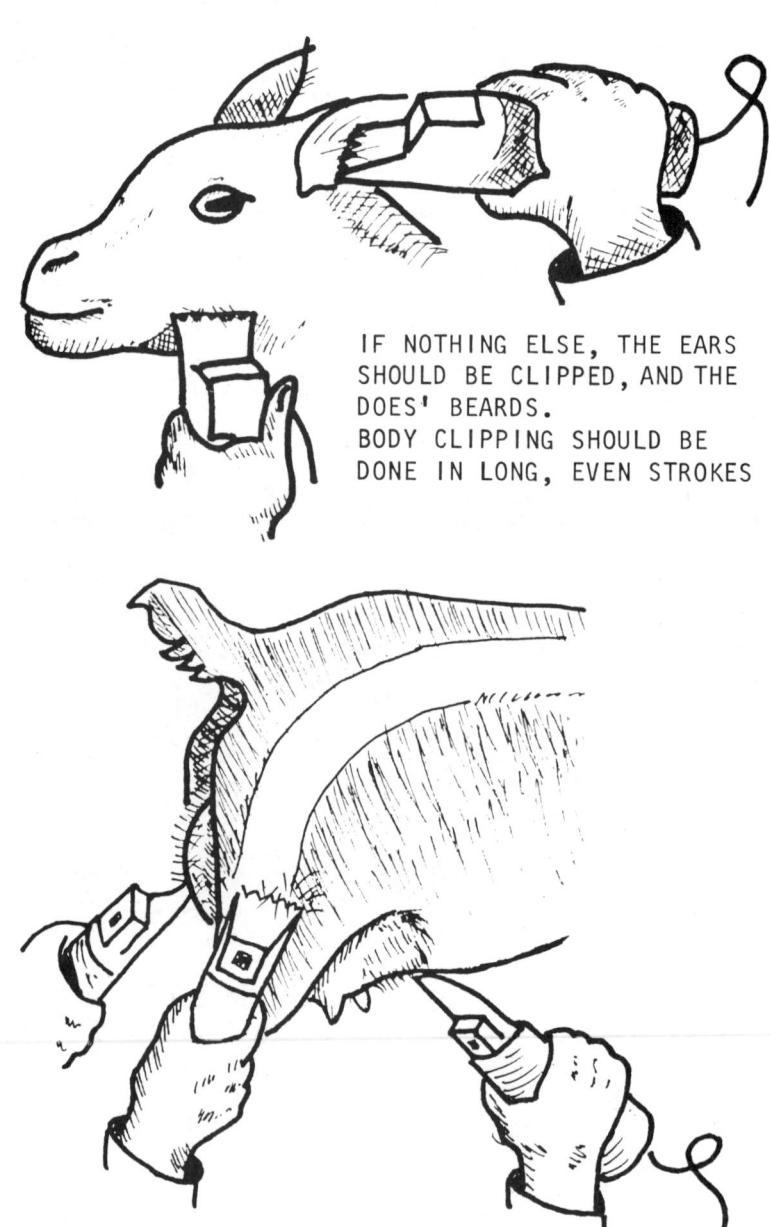

IF NOTHING ELSE, THE EARS SHOULD BE CLIPPED, AND THE DOES' BEARDS.
BODY CLIPPING SHOULD BE DONE IN LONG, EVEN STROKES

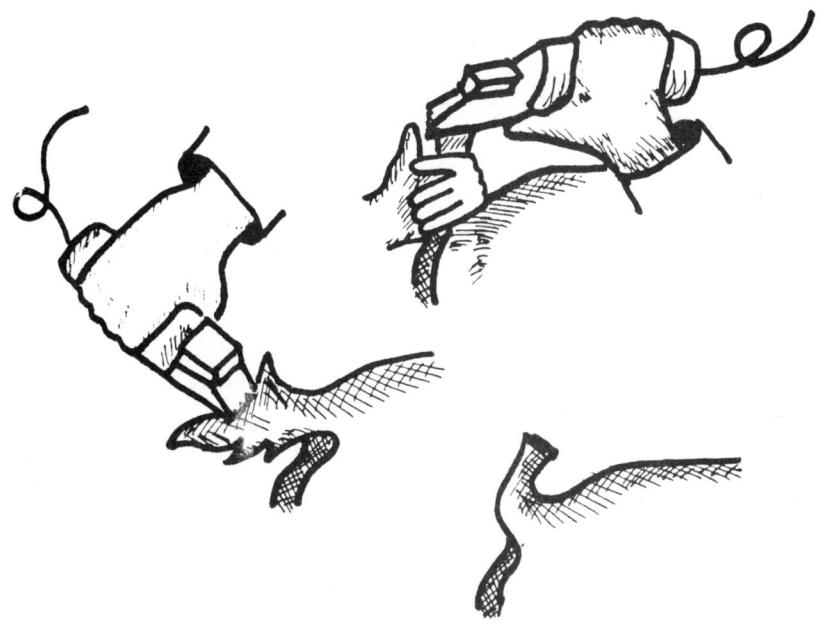

THE TAIL IS "SKIN CLIPPED" TO THE BASE AND SQUARED OFF AT THE TIP.

LEGS FROM THE HOOF TO THE KNEE SHOULD BE DONE, BUT LEGS FROM THE KNEE TO THE POINT OF ELBOW ARE OPTIONAL. TO THE THIGH IN THE REAR.

breed in any breed, but it isn't entirely reliable because condition and management affect the hair too much. Animals that are clipped might have an advantage. Clipped animals look smoother, and for that reason clipping is discussed. Clipping for show is not necessarily advocated. It's hard work, and many exhibitors do not consider it to be worth the effort. And some judges, especially in NPGA, prefer working with unclipped animals. It is wise to know a judge and the show preferences of the sanctioning organization. A disadvantage of clipping is the animal looks more refined!

For good management, milking Pygmies should be "dairy clipped" to keep the milk clean. In a dairy clip, the hair is trimmed very short with a fine blade on the clippers on the back half of the belly, the udder, the thighs, and the tail. Less hair falls in the milk pail if it is removed from these areas.

There are three ways to do clipping for show. Either the fine blade may be used over the entire animal three weeks before the show to allow some hair growth before the show, with touch-up clipping done just before show on face, legs, belly & tail; OR the clipping may all be done just before the show using the fine blade on face, belly, legs and tail, and the plucking blade on the thighs & body. Fine blade clipping on the entire body is not recommended on light animals that may sunburn.

Clipping is not recommended in winter for the health of the animal. If an owner thinks an animal needs clipping for a winter show, the "winter clip" may be used. In this, the body hair is not clipped, but the lower legs, belly, tail, and head may be done. Blending clipped parts with unclipped parts may be a problem in winter clipping.

All clipping should be done in long and even strokes running the clippers against the lay of the hair. The clippers should be held as flat against the body of the animal as possible while running. Restraining an animal in the stanchion

Two beautifully clipped and groomed AGS does from 1980-81 were bred by Loren Johnson. The black doe, Chino Acres Lil, won a one-day production star as well as showing well. The cream/gold doe with white markings, Chino Acres Taffy, was one of the first AGS master champions.

is usually all that is needed to keep her still for clipping. If the clippers start to heat up, they should be run in a mixture of half motor oil and half paint thinner to keep them running cool and smoothly.

WASHING

Pygmy owners seem to like to wash their animals for show. Light colored Pygmies probably should be washed, and any animal suspected of having external parasites should be bathed. Since goats generally don't like water, this is often a challenge. However, it's not as difficult as the job of clipping is.

For best results, the animal should be tied in a wash rack area near a hose. The area should have good drainage. The animal should be soaked well with plain water and lathered with livestock shampoo. Detergent should NEVER be used, as it can be absorbed by the animal and do real damage. The shampoo should be scrubbed in thoroughly or even brushed in, especially in stained areas. A thorough rinsing should be given the animal so no soap film is left to dull the hair. This should only be done in warm, sunny weather!

The animal must be dried completely with a soft rag or towel or by brushing so she is not chilled. If the weather is warm, as it should be, allowing the animals to romp in the sun, but not near dirt, for a while after the bath will help to dry them. The wash job should be done early enough in the day so the animals will be dry before cool evening comes, or before showing. No judge likes to handle wet animals!

Manure stains that are picked up between a bath and show time may be removed by sponging in warm water and bluing, chlorine, ammonia or even just soap. Clean animals should be put in clean pens. If washing makes the coat dry, coat conditioner may be brushed in--perhaps when the animal is still wet.

Brushing is important to all animals--especially show animals. Ideally, Pygmies should be brushed every day to eliminate dandruff and loose hair and keep the coat shiny. If this isn't possible, at least the animals being shown should be brushed often before the show, and especially on show day. Washing and brushing make the hair feel softer and silkier and the skin softer and more pliable--all advantages in the show ring.

TRAINING

Very little equipment is needed to show or train a Pygmy. A chain collar is preferred in a show with no lead. The closer the handler's hand is to the animal, the more control he will have. However, many Pygmy handlers prefer using a short lead with the collar. This is not best for good showmanship, but it helps if the Pygmy has horns. If a lead is used, it should be just long enough to keep the handler's hand away from the horns; no longer. If the Pygmy is well trained, no lead of any length should be needed.

The Pygmy should first be trained to wear a collar without fighting it. If the collar is not a hazard in the area where the Pygmy is housed, a continual wearing of it is ideal. If it is not a good idea for a Pygmy to wear the collar all the time, daily training with it will be necessary.

Pygmies in general are better behaved in the show ring than they were at the first show in 1977. Pygmies are independent little creatures, and if they can embarrass an exhibitor by lying down, or crawling, leaping, or flipping, they will! That's why training is necessary.

Daily work with leading, setting up, & standing still while the handler moves, etc. will be an advantage in the show ring. How these things are to be done will be discussed later.

Sanctioning

For the first two years of Pygmy shows, all Pygmy shows were sanctioned by both AGS and NPGA. ARF has never been involved in showing. However, the judging techniques and goals of the two organizations drifted farther and farther apart until in 1981, the AGS Board of Directors voted not to allow AGS sanctioning on any NPGA shows or shows with an NPGA judge.

In the beginning, most of the judges went to AGS judging schools and were acceptable to AGS & NPGA because of that. Then NPGA wanted its certifiers to be official judges, but AGS would not issue a blanket license unless those certifiers attended an AGS school. This was not just being picky. Goat judges are required to give reasons, and a large part of the training school has to do with how to give reasons. Without that training, an NPGA certifier simply could not do the kind of job AGS required. Besides, AGS has not yet wanted to license Pygmy judges separately from judges of the other breeds. AGS judges are trained in all breeds. Many of the AGS certifiers did attend an AGS judges' training school and were acceptable to both AGS and NPGA. But, as standards drifted farther and farther apart, most judges made a choice and went with either one organization or another.

Color was one area where judges in the two registries were not allowed to agree. AGS followed the strict interpretation of the "all colors are acceptable" statement. As time went on, the NPGA judges became more and more rigid in their interpretation of the markings descriptions, until owners of pure color Pygmies didn't feel they were getting a fair chance in NPGA shows.

Type was another area where disagreement did start to show up. This was because of the lack of definition of purpose of the Pygmy. Since the AGS constitution specifies that it registers milk goats AGS has to define the Pygmy as a milk goat. So AGS judges tend to put more emphasis on udder quality & development than NPGA judges do. NPGA judges, on the other hand, not willing to admit they may have to judge for meat type, began to put more emphasis on cobby cuteness and color markings of petstock.

Because the positions on color & purpose were so far apart, dual shows (shows sanctioned by both registries) ceased to be a reality. However, that has not kept members of either registry from enjoying the shows sanctioned by the other registry. An animal registered in AGS is often found in an NPGA show, and vice-versa, and that is good. That kind of cooperation will prevent the Pygmy breed from being fragmented into two breeds. If breeders and showmen continue to cooperate, dual shows may once again be feasible in the future. Meanwhile, there are a few dual judges who are licensed to judge in either registry, but not both at the same time.

It is not difficult to sanction a show. Some organization or individual decides to sponsor one, by furnishing facilities, judge's pay and awards, & contacts the registry about a sanction. If choice of judge meets with registry approval, and if the proper fees are paid, the registry will sanction a show. Then if the proper papers are filed with the registry after the show, the champions of that show will receive credit for their wins. It's all the rules that make a show rewarding to a breeder. It is prestigious to own a permanent or master champion. And winning is always a thrill!

When the sponsor applies to the registry, he should supply the registry with the time and place of the show, any restrictions that apply, names of all show officials as well as the judge, & the fee. Fees change so rapidly, it is best to check with a registry before applying for sanction.

Show Classes

SHOW CLASSES

Pygmy classes are not yet standardized. Some shows and fairs follow the classes set up for the larger breeds of goats, but others set their own or follow what the sheep and Angora goat classes are. Most Pygmy showmen prefer using the classes established for the larger breeds:

Junior kids--kids born April 1 to two months or so before the show in question. It is up to a show committee to determine how young the kids in the show should be. Most judges will admit there isn't much point in judging anything under eight weeks or so.

Senior kids--born January 1 to March 31 the year in which the show is held.

Junior yearlings--born July 1 to December 31 in the year before the show is held if they have not yet borne or sired kids.

Senior yearlings--born January 1 to June 30 the year before the show is held, if they haven't borne or sired kids.

Sometimes the two yearling classes are combined, but it's easier on the judge if they are separate. If the junior show is sanctioned separately from the senior show, then the champion of a junior show comes from the blue-ribbon winners of the classes listed above. If the juniors & seniors are sanctioned together, as they must be in a buck show, the winner of the competition between the blue ribbon winners of the above classes is a junior champion rather than a grand champion.

Mature or milking yearlings--born January 1 to December 31 the year before the show is held, and have borne or sired kids. A pregnant doeling with an udder, that has not yet had kids, is still considered a dry and is shown in the juniors. An unbred doe with a precocious udder is also shown in the junior classes.

Two-year-olds--animals that have freshened or sired kids and were born between January 1 and December 31 two years before the show. Animals of this age that have never produced progeny are usually ineligible to show.

Three-year-olds, born in the year three before the show and with progeny, may be shown in a separate class or be combined with the two-year-olds or the four-year-olds.

Four-year-olds may be combined with the three year-olds or with the five-year-olds, or in a small show, the last class may be called four and over.

Otherwise, the last class will be either the five and over or the six and over, depending on how the four-year-olds were handled.

If the junior and senior shows were sanctioned separately, the winner of the competition of blue ribbon winners in the above senior classes will be the grand champion senior of the show. If junior and senior shows were sanctioned together, this winner will be the senior champion, and she will compete against the junior champion for grand champion of the show. Usually a reserve in each division is also selected, and then the reserve competes against the one that didn't win grand for reserve grand champion.

An animal must win at least three such shows under at least two different judges and against an adequate amount of competition to be called a Permanent Champion (NPGA) or Master Champion (AGS). In order to earn those designations, the wins must be in official, sanctioned shows.

Group classes are a nice addition to a show, especially in moneyed fairs, and they do show how consistent a breeder is in his breeding program.

Junior get of sire is composed of three junior animals all sired by the same buck; preferably out of at least two different does.

Get of sire is composed of three animals, at least one of which is mature, all sired by the same buck. Mature animals usually have an advantage.

Sire and get is sometimes offered in a mixed buck and doe show and is composed of a buck & two offspring of any age and sex. (Unofficial!)

Dam and produce is composed of a doe and two of her daughters of any age. Mature animals usually make a stronger class if they are good does.

Produce of dam is made up of three offspring of the same mother. Mature animals will probably have an advantage, and the group will have another advantage if more than one sire is represented & if the animals are of good quality and uniform.

Breeder's trio is composed of three animals, any age, bred and owned by the exhibitor. This class is sometimes "best three," so obviously the exhibitor selects the three animals that placed highest in the individual classes.

Young herd or flock is composed of three junior animals, a buck and two does, bred and owned by the exhibitor. (Unofficial!)

Best pair, like best three, is usually selected on the basis of how the animals placed in their individual classes.

Dairy herd is composed of three or four does in milk, and it is the group that tells more than any other about the quality of the mature herd.

In addition to these group classes, special classes are often offered by shows and fairs.

Premier sire award is given to the owner or breeder (in that order depending on who's present) of the buck that has the three top-placing progeny present.

Premier exhibitor award is given to the exhibitor who won the most premium money on individual animals in a moneyed show.

Premier breeder award, based on points given for each placing, goes to the breeder of the top three to six animals, pointwise, bearing the same herd name.

Best udder is another special award that may go to the milking doe which, in the opinion of a judge, has the most ideal udder on show day.

Premiums vary from fair to fair, with small shows not offering any. However, the champions of sanctioned shows always win credits toward master or permanent championship whether money premiums are involved or not.

Some small shows & fairs offer special recreational classes for Pygmies, much like Lady's Lead in sheep. Costume classes, maze and obstacle runs are great enjoyment and increase interest in the show, but they should not be allowed to detract from the educational aspects of the show. Educating breeders, owners and the public is the first purpose of a show. Fun and enjoyment are extras!

AGS master champion, Hallcienda Bearget, P-3280, in 1992 still stands strongly at the age of nine. Championships were won at ages 2, 4, and 7.

Champions & Challengers

The champion of the day is the Pygmy which a judge determines to be the most ideal animal present in a particular show on a certain day. Each age class is placed. The first-place animals then compete for champion. If more than one sanction is purchased, more than one champion may be awarded on a single day. For example, bucks and does may not be shown against each other for championships, so if both bucks and does are shown, they must be competing for separate championships under separate sanctions.

Junior bucks do compete against senior bucks for champion of the day. Whether the junior does compete against the senior does for champion of a day is optional. Some sponsors prefer to have a single sanction, & others prefer to offer two doe sanctions so that both the junior and senior does win championships. However, a doe may only win one championship of her required three as a junior.

After each class is placed in the junior division, the first place animals all compete for junior champion. The winner of that competition is champion of the day if the junior show is on separate sanction from the senior show. Otherwise, that winner is called the junior champion. Second place animal under that winner is then called to the ring to compete with the remaining blue ribbon animals for reserve junior champion.

The same procedure is followed in the senior division, and the winner is called senior champion or grand champion if the show was separately sanctioned. If the show was not separately sanctioned then the senior champion and the junior champion compete against one another for grand champion. In some cases, even if the shows are separately sanctioned, the junior against senior competition may take place with the winner receiving the "best in show" award, even though each winner receives its own official championship leg toward permanent or master championship.

The reserve champion is selected by competing the reserve junior or reserve senior against blue ribbon winners in the proper division that did not take the division championship.

Once an animal receives three championships in official shows against adequate competition by at least two judges, and with only one win being as a junior, that animal qualifies for a permanent or master championship. Adequate competition requires that there be at least ten individuals of the breed competing for the championship, at least eight of which must be mature for bucks, in milk for does. In milk means that the does have freshened and are still milking. Dry does do not count in the "in milk" number. After an animal earns its three wins or legs, the owner applies to the registry for the permanent or master championship honor and certificate.

Some shows offer champion challenge classes, and it's a fun thing to do when there are a lot of permanent or master champions around. Challenge classes mean that the permanent or master champions present are not shown in the regular classes. Instead, when the champion of the day is selected & earns its leg, the permanent or master champions present challenge that winner for her right to be champion. If the champion of the day wins in the challenge class, she also becomes best of breed. If one of the challengers wins the challenge class the challenger becomes the best of breed, but the champion of the day still retains her win. This is a good way to keep those grand old winners in the public eye without hogging unneeded championship wins.

Entries

Premium books are so named because winners in a fair do often receive premium cash awards, & the premium books tell how much is offered. Premiums on Pygmies in larger shows may go as high as $15 on first place, and placings are paid through ninth. There is effort being made to establish Pygmies in fairs more firmly and then ask for premiums equal to what sheep and other goats get--up to $35 for a blue ribbon, with extra premiums on championships, production records, and group classes.

Entries into most shows will have to be made in advance of a date specified in the premium book. If a potential exhibitor has not received a premium book for a fair in which he wishes to show, he may address a postal card requesting one to the Livestock or Entry Department, name the fair, and name the town, state and zip code where the fair will be held. Such an address will usually suffice.

Entry information must be accurate, and most shows and fairs will check registration papers and tattoos before show day. Entry information will include the name and number of the animal to be in the show, its tattoo, birthdate, numbers and sometimes names of sire and dam, name of breeder, and the class and section numbers in which the animal will be entered. Substitutions are usually allowed if they are made at least a full day before show. Late entries usually cost a lot extra, & they can only be made by exhibitors who are already entered. It is wise to enter the full number allowed, as it is less expensive to drop a few that could not be shown than to make late entries.

Many times, fairs will request health certificates. This requirement is different in different states and at different fairs within the same state. Often, Pygmies escape the requirement, since officials do not know how to classify them. They are more often classified with the larger breeds of the dairy goats (not Angora or hair goats) than in any other category, and since dairy goats are not often carriers of serious diseases that are contagious to humans, they are often not required to have health certificates at shows within the state of origin. However, the exhibitor should always check health requirements for each show in its premium book. In many cases, all that is required is a statement from a veterinarian that the animals are in good general health and condition.

Often in out-of-state exhibiting, negative TB (tuberculosis) and brucellosis tests within thirty days of the show are required. This is seldom a problem since these two diseases are almost never found in goats in this country. Once in a while, a positive goat is found to one of these tests, but a retest usually shows negative, and the positive result can be credited to some other stress.

AGS Pygmy, Hallcienda Divine Misty, bred and owned by Stephen Divine Hall II, shows and produces well and is easy to milk.

Transportation

Pygmies are easy to transport! A few will fit with ease in the back seat of a car. A full show string, 16 to 18 animals, can easily travel in a pick-up truck if they get along. If fights must be prevented, crating the animals separately will work, but fewer are carried that way. A few animals to be shown some distance away can be flown to the show. Most commercial airlines are usually cooperative about shipping goats.

No matter how the animals are transported, every effort should be made to keep them comfortable.

The vehicle should be well bedded with straw. If space allows, and if the journey is long, feed and water should be available in the vehicle. A covered vehicle is best in cold or wet weather, but the open top and slatted side offer ventilation that is needed in warmer weather.

On very long journeys, if the animals are traveling by truck, provision should be made for small exercise pens where they can be released at least twice a day during milking times. A stop is a good idea even for milkers that are nursing kids and not being milked, as kids will often not nurse in a moving vehicle.

If possible, the journey should be planned so that animals arrive at the fair at least one day before the show, or by the time the premium book says they must be there, to give the goats time to rest and adjust to new surroundings before they are shown.

Under any circumstances, showing is traumatic to the animals. Travel and showing & accompanying stresses make the Pygmy susceptible to a variety of diseases and infections, and showing with animals from other areas introduces the infections, so conditions are prime for sick goats.

Shipping fever has long been a problem to all kinds of animals when they travel. The section on vaccinations discusses one that will protect the animals from this disease.

Whether the animals are vaccinated or not, a pre-travel preventive injection of long-acting Bicillin is not a bad idea. In addition, some antibiotics should be taken along in case the animals begin to show symptoms of infections while they are at the show. Respiratory infections are most commonly encountered at a show.

Kaopectate is an excellent medication to take to a show. The change in water often causes bad cases of scours in the goats, and sometimes in the exhibitors. A bottle of Kaopectate is a blessing. Doses with Kaopectate are unknown. The recommended human dose doesn't do much good in a goat so at least doubling it is better. Much higher doses than that can be given without harm.

Hallcienda Easter, P-6480, has won recent AGS championships. She exhibits the heavy muscling of her grandsire MCH Morris's Bear. Her horns allowed her to escape when a coyote ate her entire left thigh. Her recovery left only a small indentation, even though all flesh was gone to the tendon.

Show Equipment

Every vehicle headed for a show will carry in it a "tack box" loaded with all the equipment and personal effects the exhibitor might need during a stay at a fair. The tack box should be strong and well-constructed, and it should lock with a padlock so things will be safe. Often the tack box holds valuable equipment.

The following equipment should be taken to a show to help make the animals more comfortable and to keep them groomed and give them the care needed:

antibiotics	feeders
brushes	hoof trimmers
clippers	livestock shampoo
cloths or sponges	portable stanchion
coat dressing	syringe & needles
collars	tie chains
feed	water buckets
kaopectate	stop-blood powder

The equipment in the following list will help keep the exhibitor comfortable at the show or fair:

books or cards	flashlight
cot	sleeping bag
chair	soap & toiletries
clean clothing	towels
(including show uniform)	

Other equipment needed to keep the pen areas attractive and clean follows:

broom	milk pail
business cards	nails
display signs	pitch fork
hammer	pliers & wire

In addition to all of that, the exhibitor will have to take his registration papers so they can be checked, and his premium book will help him figure his winnings, check show times and classes so animals will be to the ring on time.

Arrival at Show

When the exhibitor arrives at the fair, his first stop will be the livestock office. There he will find out where his assigned pens are.

At the pen area, several things will have to be done, and their order depends upon how much has already been done, how long the trip has been, and what conditions the goats are in after the trip.

Straw will have to be put in the pens for bed material. Feeders and water buckets will have to be put in the pens and filled. Animals will have to be unloaded from the vehicles and distributed among the pens in such a way that fighting will be minimized. Usually exhibitors will help one another load and unload the animals as this reduces the work load for everyone.

Then the display at the pen area is arranged. The exhibit should be neat, attractive, and eye-catching. Some large fairs offer cash awards to the top herdsmen. In addition, most Pygmy exhibitors take pride in presenting their animals in an attractive way to an interested public. Every effort should be made to help overcome the "smelly billy-goat, can-eating" image the public often has of the goat.

Now comes another trip to the livestock office to check papers and pick up admission passes. This is the time, too to make any substitutions, scratches, or additions to the show entries. It is also a good idea to check the show schedule to see if there have been any changes. It is frustrating to go through all the preparatory work & then miss showing an animal because of a revised show schedule.

If this is a fair that checks all tattoos, it will be done between this visit at the office and show time. All ears should be clean for tattoo reading. If the tattoo cannot be easily read, even in bright sunlight, shining a flashlight or high intensity lamp through the ear from the back side, usually brings out the tattoo clearly. If tattoo cannot be read, it should not be redone in exactly the same area as the first one. Tattoos sometimes fade and return, and if this happens after retattooing, a double image, resulting in an illegible tattoo will result. In retattooing, the second tattoo must be put in a different area of the ear from the first.

During the stay at the fair, one of the main jobs of the exhibitor is to keep the pens clean. It is difficult enough for some fair-goers walking into an enclosed barn without having to cope with additional odors of dirty pens. Besides the image of the goat needs to be protected better than that.

The image of cleanliness and sanitation at milking time is especially important at fairs. An animal needs to be milked as regularly at a fair as she is at home. Sanitary methods include putting the doe on a clean stanchion, washing her udder with a clean cloth moistened with clean water and milking into a clean metal pail. If a doe is difficult to manage at milking time, an injection of antihistamine 20 to 30 minutes before milking may take the tickle out of her teats and keep her from being an embarrassment.

Between arrival at the fair and show day, an exhibitor will keep up the grooming practices he started during the fitting period. This includes the daily brushings and feedings. No additional clipping should be done at fairs. This should be done at home, but if touch-ups are needed, they should be done when spectators are not around, & all hair clippings should be cleaned up fast.

If an animal got dirty during the trip, bath time will have to be repeated before show day. A wash rack will probably be available at a fair, & the animal can be tied and washed there. Shampooing should be done the day before the show, as no judge enjoys handling a wet animal. If a complete bath is not necessary, but the goat has some spots that need to be removed, this may be done the day of the show with a sponge or cloth or brush moistened with soapy water or water containing chlorox, ammonia or bluing.

Before the show Pygmies may need to have the horns and hoofs oiled. Mineral oil works well, & the exhibitor needs only to rub the oil on with a soft cloth and polish it with a dry cloth. Oil makes the horns and hoofs look dark and shiny, a nice touch in the show ring. However, neither of the horns nor hoofs should be dyed or painted, & the kneeling pads on the knees should never be colored or painted. These practices are too artificial, and coloring the knee pads alerts a judge to inspect the knees more closely. Goats who use their legs correctly must have knee pads, and if they are missing or painted over, the judge will suspect lameness and discriminate accordingly.

1992 NPGA Permanent Champion, Critter Country Lisa, 8895F, bred by Don and Audree Anderson and owned by Christine and Tom Hallquest, also shows fairly well in AGS shows.

Show Day

Does are not milked on show day, so morning chores include just feeding and spot-cleaning of the coat. The exhibitor may want to brush coat conditioner into the hair of the animal before show, but the coat should not be made oily. If hoofs were trimmed at the time the coat was clipped, or within a week or so of the show, no additional hoof trimming will have to be done show day. The hoofs will probably have to be cleaned (manure removed), and they may be oiled.

Milkers should be checked to see that, in skipping the morning milking, the udders are not becoming too strutted. If a doe shows evidence of producing too much milk to be held until show time, the exhibitor may wish to relieve pressure by removing some of the milk. If a doe is slightly unbalanced in the udder, the exhibitor should remove milk from the heavy half.

Unfortunately, there is not much that can be done for a doe that is not bagging up well due to stresses of the trip. Water intake is important to milk production. Using molasses in the water at home before the trip and adding molasses to the water at the show will encourage does to keep up their water intake because the flavor will be familiar. Salt at a fair should not be neglected for the same reason. A doe with salt drinks more water and makes more milk and barrel.

After morning chores and grooming of the animals is complete, the final step is to prepare the exhibitor. All exhibitors should wear white uniforms, but a white shirt with colored slacks may be acceptable in some shows. If the shirt has the herd emblem on the back of it, the show uniform is even more attractive, and the advertising is good, too. This kind of showtime uniformity is good for the image of the Pygmy.

The contest begins the minute the class is called to the ring. Often judges notice important points while the animals are being led to the ring, so proper leading procedures should begin as soon as the animal leaves the pen.

The handler should walk by the head of his animal, on the left side, holding the collar with his right hand. It is important to be on time to the class, not keeping the judge and other exhibitors waiting for one person and one animal. Tie chains to hold animals ring-side will help.

The attitude of the exhibitor is important. A judge appreciates one who always knows where the judge is and what he wants without appearing to stare at the judge. The exhibitor should be polite and respond quickly and inconspicuously when the judge requests him to move. The exhibitor is appreciated who can answer questions, too. Often a judge likes to know the exact age of an animal, or the freshening date. This kind of talking to a judge is acceptable.

It is very bad practice for the exhibitor to make his opinions about the judge & judging known in the ring or near the ring. If the judge has done something that displeases the exhibitor, the exhibitor will be better off to forget it. Arguing with the judge, making audibly unfavorable comments about the judge to other exhibitors, and showing displeasure in facial expressions are very bad practices. It also does no good to share a discontent with other exhibitors, even out of the hearing of the judge, as word reaches him anyway.

Asking questions after the class is placed & reasons given, and accepting the answers dispassionately are acceptable practices. Questions will be more accurately answered if they are asked before the class of animals leaves the ring. It is acceptable to thank the judge for his job. No comment is necessary if the exhibitor was not pleased.

Basic Showing

Pygmies are not as easy to teach to lead well as are other breeds because they are more aggressive and playful, but a well-behaved animal always shows better and has an advantage in the show ring. The exhibitor will have better control of his animal if he uses just a collar held high up under the chin of his animal. It is to the benefit of the exhibitor not to use a lead with the collar, but if a short one is needed to keep the hands and horns apart, many judges may not object.

Animals should be taught to lead well. When an animal is led into the ring, she and the exhibitor will walk in a clock-wise direction around the ring. If the judge stands in the center of a ring no special maneuvering by the handler will be necessary. He simply keeps the animal between himself and the judge. However, if the judge stands in the corner of the ring or to one side to have a better view of the rear of the animals, the exhibitor will have to cross in front of his animal to lead on the side away from the judge. The approximate, relative positions of judge, exhibitor, and animal are in the diagram below of a class of Pygmies circling the ring.

Circling the ring--the exhibitors cross in front of their animals as needed.

Pygmies are so little, it's always a temptation to step over them when it is necessary to go to the other side. This is a bad practice. Not only does it look bad, but it's a good way to lose control of the animal or get gored in the groin by a tossed horn. Walking behind an animal never looks good because it puts the animal in an awkward position. True, the exhibitor feels that way crossing in front, but the judge is watching the animal, not the exhibitor.

The exhibitor will also have to move to the other side of his animal if, while standing in a line side-by-side, the judge moves. The following line-ups show about where the exhibitors should be as a judge changes his position in relation to the position of the animals.

Exhibitors must stay out of the line of view of the judge.

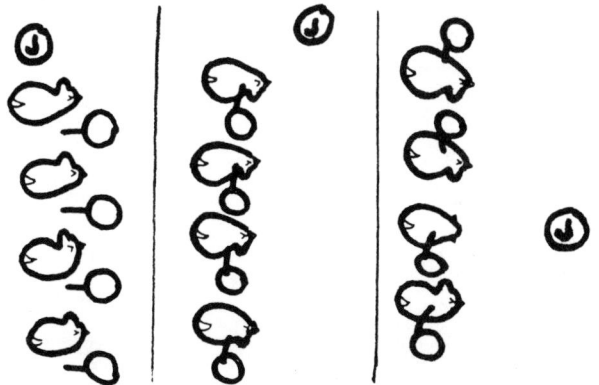

Notice that when the judge stands at one end of the line, the exhibitors should all be at the heads of their animals.

SHOWING

The animals should be trained not to move just because the handlers do. Whenever the handler is to move from one side of his animal to the other, he should cross in front of his animal. Crossing behind an animal looks awkward because pressure is exerted on the throat of the animal which causes it to stop, turn, scrunch up or lift its head too high.

When the judge requests the animals to stop walking, whether they are to be lined up head-to tail or side-by-side, enough room should be left between animals to allow the judge to walk in between them without bumping one another, and to allow for easy movement when another animal is brought into the line. Crowding another exhibitor's animal in the show ring is poor sportsmanship. Exhibitors already standing in an assigned position should make room for animals the judge may reposition near them.

Crowding the judge is also poor sportsmanship, and it makes it difficult for him to see animals that are too close to him. The line is best formed a good viewing distance from where a judge is standing.

SETTING UP AN ANIMAL

Pygmies should be posed with all four legs set squarely under them. If any stretching is to be done, say to level up the rump, it should be done moderately, or the Pygmy will look too long for the breed. Proportions will be off.

To square up the front feet, the hand of the showman may be run over the shoulder of the animal with the middle finger pointing straight down making a line through the knee and pastern. If a leg is so set, it is in the proper position. A leg that needs to be moved may simply be picked up and replaced where the exhibitor wants it. A Pygmy is small enough there should be no problem for any exhibitor with this technique. The front legs should be set straight under the animal, but they should be spread apart some to accentuate the natural width of the animal's chest. Showmanship was established for the purpose of helping an animal to always look its best!

To assist the judge in seeing the animal at its best at all times, the legs nearest the judge should be set first--front legs if the judge is at the front of the animal, but back legs first if the judge is at the rear of the animal. If a side view is the judge's desire, it will be easier to square up the animal if the front legs are set first.

The hind feet should not be stretched to the rear as they are in the other breeds, as Pygmies are not supposed to look long as the others are. The hind feet should be set naturally so that a straight line would pass through the pin bone, & the hock, & the pastern. Stretching rear legs back may tend to bring a steeper rump more in line with the topline, but the total appearance of the Pygmy might suffer. The hind legs should spread apart to show rear width, unless this makes the udder look poorly attached. Width should be accentuated in a dry doe, and also in a milker, if the udder appearance does not suffer.

Often a judge will rock the animal from side to side to check udder attachments. Keeping the hind legs a little closer together will prevent udder swing, indicating more udder support. Hind legs may be moved by picking them up & placing them as are the front legs. If more control to prevent kicking is needed, the hind legs should be grasped just above the hock, with some pressure put on the tendon at that point.

If an animal moves badly out of position, it is best to reposition her just as if the judge had asked that she be moved to a different place. The animal should be led forward out of line, (down to the new position if so instructed), back through the line (this would be a U-turn if the same position in line is maintained), with another U-turn at the back of the line, and back into position in the line. Since Pygmies are four-legged animals, it is best to give them plenty of turning room. Handlers often short-turn their animals because they don't realize that those with four legs can not turn as sharply as those with two legs. Pushing an animal into position is usually bad practice. Leading is better.

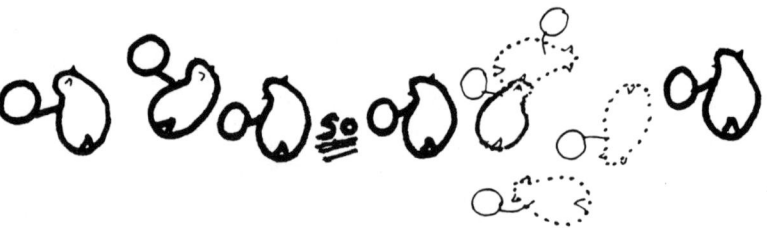

The illustration shows how an animal should be led back into position rather than pushing it from the side. Placing each leg separately to reposition a Pygmy is also acceptable.

The exhibitor always walks forward when he is leading an animal. He may look back at the judge for further instructions, but he should not walk backwards. Cattle showmen walk backwards, but the animals are not small enough to trip over, either. For more complete control, the Pygmy should always be turned toward the handler. In other words, at the peak of the turn, the animal should face the handler; the exhibitor should not be at the rear of his animal.

SHOWING OUT FAULTS

It is the job of the exhibitor to show his animal to her fullest advantage at all times. That means the exhibitor has to know the faults of his animal. And the exhibitor should employ methods of showing that can inconspicuously cover those faults whenever possible.

For example, since it is not best to stretch out a Pygmy with a steep rump, pinching the third vertebra in front of the hip bones usually will encourage an animal to bring up the rump.

Or, if the shoulders tend to wing out (separate too far from the body wall), spreading the front feet farther apart will bring the shoulders in more tightly and make the withers look sharper, too. A Pygmy needs to look wide, so this spreading of legs is quite acceptable.

If the topline tends to dip, bringing the hind legs closer to the front legs will help raise it, as will posing the animal with its head a little lower. Since Pygmies should be short, the method of moving legs is very good. Since Pygmies tend to hold their heads too low anyway, the second method might not do as well. Most animals will also respond to a little tickle on her tummy behind the heart girth to bring her topline up. This method is best not used unless the animal is very deep, or it tends to make the Pygmy look shallow, which is not good.

If an animal tends to "hock in" in the rear, that is, if she stands "cow hocked" with her hocks closer together than other parts of her hind legs, the exhibitor can help to correct this when the hind legs are placed. With a firm grasp over the tendon above the hocks, the hocks can be inconspicuously turned out as the handler sets the feet down. However, these faults cannot be corrected on the move, which is why so many judges do so much of the job while the animals are walking.

The handler should try to appear natural and inconspicuous, no matter how hard he is working to show his animal. Such practice and attitude are usually rewarded in the placings.

If, in the course of showing, the judge asks the exhibitor to stop a particular practice, for example, tickling the tummy, it is best for the exhibitor to stop. The judge has a better view of the animal than the exhibitor does, and the work of the exhibitor may be making the animal look too unnatural.

If an animal is well trained, it will take a proper show stance whenever the handler stops, but most animals will need some placement in the ring. It is usually preferred that the exhibitor pick up each foot individually and place it where he wants it. This is easy to do with a Pygmy, because it is no problem reaching over an animal.

Christy's Critters Billie Jean, P-6732, 1220F, bred and owned by Christine and Thomas Hallquest, is a rare AGS Master and NPGA Permanent champion!

Showmanship

Every exhibitor should learn good showmanship whether or not he ever intends to enter a class of showmanship. Good showmanship should be used in every class in every show. Good showmanship is a matter of knowing the rules and maneuvers, but it is more than that, too. A good showman has a kind of charisma that is transmitted to the animal that makes even a poor-looking animal shape up and look its best. It's uncanny and probably can't be defined or explained.

According to the showmanship score card, good showmanship is 40% appearance of the animal (that is grooming, health, cleanliness--not conformation) 10% appearance of the exhibitor, and 50% on showing ability.

Animal appearance is based on healthy condition (10 points), clean and well-groomed head and hoofs (10 points), neatly dehorned or clean horns and clipped coat (at least feet, tail and head, for 10 points), and cleanliness, especially of feet & legs and tail area, nose and ears (10 points).

Appearance of the exhibitor is judged on neatness and cleanliness and the appropriate uniform (preferably white with matching shoes and belt). If it is the policy of the show or fair not to require a uniform, this category is ignored, except that a showman should be clean and neat.

Leading the animal is worth 10 points. When entering the ring, leading should be done at normal pace in a clockwise direction around the ring. The exhibitor should walk on the animal's left, or on the side away from the judge, holding the collar in the hand nearest the animal, with the collar as high up under the chin as possible. The hand directly on the collar is preferred, although a short lead may be used if the animal has horns. The exhibitor should walk forward--never backward. The animal should respond readily with her head held high enough to show style and grace and attractive carriage. Again, the collar, without a lead, held high up on the neck, right under the chin, gives the handler better control of the animal.

Posing and showing the animal is 15 points. The animal must always be between the judge & the exhibitor. The animal should be posed as described earlier, and it will show better if the front feet are placed on an incline. This position is best for showing straight topline, level rump, & angularity. When an exhibitor is asked to move his animal, he pulls forward out of line, down the front of the line to the new position, back through the line, makes a U-turn behind the line & pulls the animal into place.

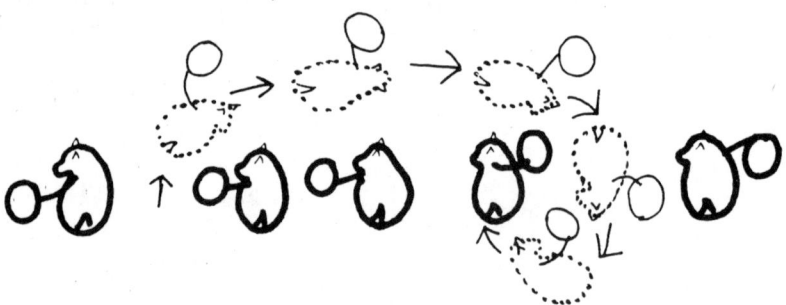

The diagram shows how a move in position is done.

The exhibitor should be careful not to over-show, fuss with or pet his animal unnecessarily, or maneuver the animal without good cause.

For 15 points, the exhibitor must recognize the faults of his animal and show the animal all the time to its best advantage, trying to overcome those faults.

For another 10 points, the exhibitor must be able to show poise, naturalness, alertness & courtesy. It is important that the exhibitor watch the judge and the animal both so that he is always aware of what the judge wants and how his animal looks. He should not be distracted by things outside the ring, and he will continue to show well to the end of the class when everyone is dismissed.

Showing well to the end is important. It is disheartening to the judge to go to the microphone to give his reasons on his showmanship class, only to see his first choice showing everyone he doesn't really belong there.

POINTERS ON SHOWING

When it is necessary for the exhibitor to go to the opposite side of his animal or change direction, it will give him more control of the situation if he turns his animal toward himself. The illustration below shows how. The animal is being led from left to right, is turned, and comes back from right to left.

If the animals are lined up head-to-tail & the judge requests a change of position between any two animals, the animal nearer the front of the line is led out of line to the side away from the judge, & the rear animal is taken to the forward position & just led into place. Then the first forward anim- is led back past the new position, turned, and led into the new spot. This is illustrated below.

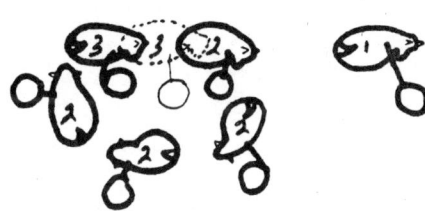

In many ways, showmanship is difficult for a judge to judge, partly because very few maneuvers a judge puts the exhibitors through have been defined procedurally. Many judges feel that showmanship should be left to the creativity of each exhibitor, but maneuvers that require two handlers to work together should be defined. Some common ones are defined here.

If a judge requests two animals to trade places when the animal are lined up side-by-side, there is an easy, smooth way to accomplish such a difficult maneuver. Both exhibitors walk their animals forward side by side and turn to the right so the exhibitor on the left follows the one on the right. Then the two circle, one behind the other, clockwise, through the line, and back into their new positions. The following diagram may help.

Often a judge will request that two animals walk side by side so the judge can compare them. Since the judge is interested in seeing the animals walk as closely together as possible, the exhibitors will walk on the outside of the pair of animals regardless of where the judge stands. In most cases, however, the judge will position himself where he can see the animals from the rear as they walk away from him. The diagram that follows shows two animals walking side by side from left to right with the handlers on the outsides of the pair. On the turn, each handler turns his animal toward him so the two animals have their rumps to one another. On the return walk from right to the left, again the animals are side by side and the exhibitors are on the outsides of the pair.

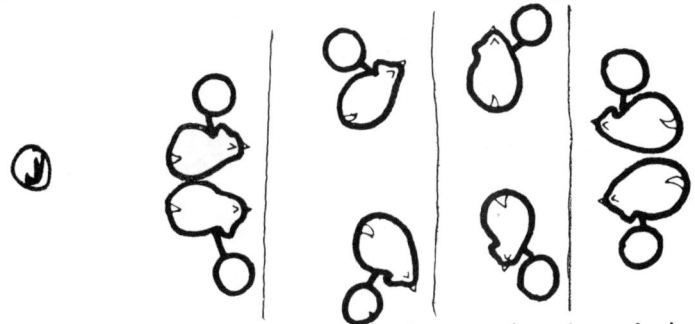

When the class is placed to suit the judge, he will give reasons for making his placings. A judge will usually try to make it understood that every animal or showman in the class has merit, & he will try to point out strong points in each. A usual way for a judge to give reasons is to compare each pair of animals or showmen. Comparison should make the points clearer than simple, individual description.

If the exhibitor has any questions about the placing, the judge should be asked immediately and before the class leaves the ring. Questions are best if they are specific. No judge likes to hear, "Why did my animal go last?" after he has given a lot of reasons explaining why.

It is a wise exhibitor who accepts the opinion of the judge without argument or undue comment for what it is--the opinion of a trained individual. No matter how many training sessions judges attend, every judge will "see" an animal a little bit differently from every other judge.

A wise exhibitor also realizes that animals & competitions change, and just because an animal is champion one day doesn't mean she will be the next day, or even that she should be.

AN EARLY PYGMY BUCK,

RON'S LITTLE CARL, BRED BY RON JOHNSON AND OWNED BY NANCY LAKE, WAS SHOWN ONCE AT THE AGE OF SEVEN AND HE WON CHAMPION. HE WAS ONLY $16\frac{1}{2}$ INCHES TALL, AND ALTHOUGH VERY SLIGHT, SHOWED EXCELLENT WIDTH, ESPECIALLY FROM THE REAR.

    Carl had an exciting experience during his life. He lived on his Southern California goat farm surrounded by lovely does--La Manchas on one side, Nubians on another, and Pygmies on another.

    One winter it flooded! Many of the smaller animals were lost. Many of the larger ones got sick. But Carl made the best of a very bad situation. He was seen standing on a pallet that floated across his pen on the wind-stirred ripples. As his pallet approached one side of his pen, he would blub-blub-blub at the nifty Nubian does. When he drifted to the other side, he'd do his blub-blub-blubs for the lovely La Manchas ♀, and he didn't ignore his own herd when he coasted to their side.

    Now that's an adaptable buck! Carl died of enterotoxemia at the age of nine. Ron's herd traced to Ruhe and Big Bear animals, & Big Bear traced back to Oklahoma City Zoo. Carl was of the Ruhe stock entirely.

After Show

A feeling of relaxation usually hits exhibitors after a show. Now the results of all preparations are known, and people can concentrate on a lot of other things. If it is a one-day show, of course, there is packing, loading and cleaning-up to do.

If it is a longer fair, chores & pen-cleaning still have to be done regularly, and the display has to be kept looking neat and attractive, but now the exhibitors have time to visit, see other parts of the fair, have parties, or whatever they want to do to relax. On the surface most owners of Pygmies seem to get along no matter how competitive they are about their animals or their registries.

If the animals are not to be shown again soon they should be eased back into herd life. Change from show circuit to herd living should be made gradually to reduce the chances of adverse effects on the animals.

If animals are headed for another show soon, the exhibitor will do well to learn from the last show which animals need more work, more training, more conditioning, less conditioning, and plan a schedule for the show string from his learning.

Showing is often the high point of many Pygmy owners' year. It gives them a chance to have their animals compared with others in the area, & this may give a breeder some ideas on where to make changes in his breeding program or what lines he might want to bring into his herd.

Showing also gives a breeder a chance to put his animals, of which he is understandably proud, before the public and other breeders. Showing gives a breeder the opportunity to exhibit a lot more than his animals.

He is, actually, exhibiting the effects of his management and fitting practices, as well as the genetic potential of his stock. He is also displaying his ability in selection, both for show and for the breeding stock he keeps.

Whether or not a breeder shows his bucks, he is showing the strengths and weaknesses of those bucks in their daughters.

In addition, show premiums often give a goat owner a chance to add to his income from his Pygmies.

Therefore, when show season arrives, selection, fitting and showing are all evident in every show. Showmanship is not the least important of these three aspects. A good showman can raise the placing of his animal several places sometimes, & a poor showman certainly makes the job especially difficult for the judge.

A sincere breeder takes pride in always doing the best he can in all aspects connected with his herd---because he probably loves his animals.

1992--That love of animals still directs Pygmy breeders no matter what direction they go. People say there's an AGS type Pygmy (angular, dairy, colorful) and an NPGA type Pygmy (cobby, heavy), the animals have not changed drastically. Animals that have been clipped, as on page 91, or groomed for smoothness will look more "AGS," and animals that have been full-fed and fluff-dried will look more "NPGA," but a Pygmy is still a Pygmy.

It is such an endearing animal people are crossing it with other breeds to manufacture new breeds with Pygmy characteristics. Pygora Breeders Assn., 16619 S. Bradley Rd., Oregon City, OR 97045, works with the Angora cross. Kinder Goat Breeders Assn., P.O. Box 1575 Snohomish, WA 98291-1575 promotes the Nubian cross. International Dairy Goat Registry, Rt. 1 Box 165-A, Rossville, GA 30741, handles these and Alpine and other crosses.

What is a Nigerian Dwarf?

Nigerian Dwarves are registered separately from Pygmies in both AGS and IDGR. Whether they are really separate breeds is highly debatable, but the precedent was set with Sables/Saanens and Oberhaslies/Alpines for registering in separate herdbooks animals of the same breed that have a slightly different standard.

Nigerian Dwarf is mentioned as a synonym for Pygmy on page eight of this book. The terms probably are synonymous, but since Pygmy breeders bred their animals in extreme directions from the original standard and intent presented to AGS in 1975, there appears to be a need for some way to include dwarf goats that have not been bred for extreme "cobbiness."

Page eight also refers to three classes of West African Dwarf found on that continent. It has been suggested that the larger type is our Pygmy, the medium type is our Nigerian Dwarf, and the small type, or Toy, has not yet been imported. Since that surmise was made, AGS has found it necessary to increase the height standard on the Nigerian Dwarf buck, indicating that, perhaps, the Dwarf is the largest type, and the Pygmy is the medium type.

Or, perhaps the Nigerian Dwarf breeders are breeding in the opposite direction from the Pygmy breeders and manufacturing a breed intermediate between Pygmies and the larger breeds. Time will tell what will happen with this new breed.

Meanwhile, the IDGR and AGS herdbooks are still open to new additions. Both will take animals from existing Pygmy herdbooks, as well as other, unknown animals that meet the standard and produce progeny that meet the standard. AGS extended its 1992 closure date and now intends to close Nigerian Dwarf herdbooks in 1997. IDGR maintains open herdbooks for animals of unknown ancestry, and after "grading up" these animals' offspring to about 95% pure by breeding to purebred Nigerian bucks, progeny may be entered into the purebred book.

Its name and early writings on the Nigerian Dwarf classify it, like the Pygmy, an achondroplastic dwarf, and the IDGR breed standard concurs. However, the AGS breed standard for the Nigerian Dwarf which follows does not reflect that definition. The standard says:

"The Nigerian Dwarf is a miniature dairy breed of West African origin. Its conformation is similar to that of the larger breeds. The parts of the body are in balanced proportion; an animal with a disproportionately large head, or one with a relatively large body on short legs, is not acceptable. The nose is straight, though there may be a small break or stop at the level of the eyes. The ears are upright.

"The coat is soft, with hair that is short to medium length. The desired height is sixteen inches to eighteen inches for does, and eighteen to twenty inches for bucks, with no minimum for either sex.

"Any color or combination of colors is acceptable, though silver agouti is a moderate fault.

"Breed-specific disqualifications are curly coat, roman nose, pendulous ears, and bucks over twenty-three inches or does over twenty-one inches at withers."

The IDGR standard sounds somewhat different: "The Nigerian Dwarf goat is one of two dwarf or miniature goat breeds currently in America. It

Goodwood River Avon, above, an AGS reserve champion gold Dwarf doe was bred by Kathy Claps and is owned by Shaula Parker. When comparing her with the doe below, her younger age and clipped condition should be considered. Pine Cone Valley 34, below, is an IDGR gold Dwarf bred and owned by Robert Johnson.

is a true achondroplastic dwarf of West African origin, genetically small in size, with a body larger in proportion to leg length than is found in other breeds, except the...Pygmy, the other miniature breed.

"Nigerian Dwarves may be described briefly as miniature dairy goats, and as such, they differ in basic body type from Pygmy goats, which ideally are of a blocky, compact, heavily-muscled structure. Dwarves are short and soft-coated, with fine textured and pliable, loose skin, flat and flinty bone, refined structure, angularity, and general openness. They are bright-eyed, alert, companionable, and hardy."

The standard goes on at length describing colors, brown, black, and gold, and markings, which should be random and irregular. It describes the coat as short and straight instead of full as the Pygmy standard does, and Nigerian bucks should not have the heavy beard and mane seen in Pygmies.

The head of the Nigerian should be medium to long instead of short as in the Pygmy, and the face should be flat or slightly dished, or "similar to that of an Alpine dairy goat, in miniature."

"Dwarves are genetically horned....Horns to be well-spaced, curving outward, semi-triangular or ovoid in cross-section. In bucks with several years of horn growth, horns should extend upward from the head, turn outward, and then up again at the ends or tips. Semicircular horns are standard in does; a minor fault in bucks. Horns that are parallel, incurving, touching, crossing, and/or closely-set are faults...." The same horn standards are in the IDGR Pygmy standard.

"The neck is longer than that of the Pygmy," but descriptions of body, feet and legs, mammary, and reproductive system are essentially the same as in the Pygmy.

"The Dwarf breed is slightly smaller than the Pygmy breed, and size is one primary differential." Height at the withers is from sixteen to nineteen inches for does and seventeen to twenty inches for bucks. Maximum sizes are twenty-two inches for bucks and twenty-one inches for does, and there are no minimum sizes. The IDGR standard goes on to say that "Dwarves tend to grow more slowly early in life than Pygmies."

Both American Goat Society and International Dairy Goat Registry have score cards for judging the Nigerian Dwarf. A comparison of the two score cards is shown, and again one can see why dual shows are improbable.

	AGS		IDGR	
	Does	Bucks	Does	Bucks
Appearance	14	20	included	below
Head	8	10	6	6
Color	0	0	7	10
Markings	0	0	5	5
Horns	0	0	4	6
Neck	3	5	3	4
Shoulders	5	8	9	10
Chest	10	13	7	10
Barrel	10	10	8	10
Skin/Ribs	4	7	10	12
Flank	0	0	2	3
Back	included	above	5	5
Rump	10	10	4	4
Feet/Legs	10	17	10	12
Mammary	26	0	20	0
Testicles	0	0	0	3

Fresa, a "caramel" colored Nigerian Dwarf doe, AGS D-11925, owned by Laura Beers.

Bonnie Abrahamson's J.J. #2, the first Nigerian Dwarf in any registry, 1982, was owned by Robert Johnson. This buck was a first generation offspring from an original import.

Goodwood Nelson, an AGS Dwarf bred by Kathy Claps and owned by Florence Sunni has won at least one reserve.

Nigerian-Pygmy Comparison

After the AGS/NPGA split in 1979, AGS set up local certification committees and held certification days so local committees could certify many Pygmies at one time in person. To one such certification day, Mrs. Bonnie Abrahamson brought several does which she consistently called Nigerian Dwarves. The certifiers accepted them into the Pygmy herdbook because they met the Pygmy standard, even though they were a little more refined and had "plainer" heads than the "ideal." However, Mrs. Abrahamson was not satisfied being in the Pygmy herdbooks with her Nigerian Dwarves, especially after NPGA started breeding for heavier, cobbier animals than were originally presented to AGS.

Meanwhile, a Mr. Heabert Wood in Indiana, acquired a brown-and-white herd of animals similar to Mrs. Abrahamson's black and white ones. They were rejected by NPGA because of color, and AGS was not approached. Mr. Robert Johnson, working on the breed standards committee for International Dairy Goat Registry, was contacted, and he convinced IDGR to open a Nigerian Dwarf registry in 1980 for animals like Abrahamson's and Wood's. Similar herds were located in Florida (Sue Alfano), and Washington (Jeff Hatch), all of which had been maintained as rather closed herds, and none of which had tried to have their animals certified by either AGS or NPGA either through ignorance of the program or belief their animals were not acceptable. All had originated from a "traveling zoo." Patricia Freeman of Ontario Canada bought bucks from Bonnie Abrahamson and does from Iris Watson, who'd been active in Pygmies in Michigan, and established Dwarves in Canada.

IDGR herdbooks were opened and placed an emphasis on maintaining the three color lines discovered. A gold-and-white line existed besides the other two. AGS also opened a Nigerian Dwarf herdbook in 1983 because, even though color was not an issue for AGS Pygmy breeders, type was.

Compared with Pygmies, Dwarves show the same size head, larger for body size than full-sized goats. Beyond that, although the animals are very similar, one can find differences. Generally, Dwarves have narrower muzzles and more level faces. They have slightly longer necks and legs, especially in the cannon bones, perhaps more refined bone, and their barrels are not as wide or deep as those of the Pygmies. Where most Pygmy breeders have limited themselves to the standard blacks, agoutis, and caramels described by NPGA, even though AGS says that's not necessary, many of the pretty white, cream, red,

IDGR's Pine Cone Valley Dot of Robert Johnson's herd, illustrates the Schwartzhal pattern.

and chocolate colors that were in the earliest Pygmy shows, are now in the Dwarf herds. Some colorful Pygmy herds still exist, but they seldom show.

There is evidence that all colors exist in the West African Dwarves, and the Pygmy in America may be the loser because of the discrimination against these colors. Color aside, American breeders of both Pygmies and Nigerian Dwarves seem to be going in opposite directions with their animals through selective breeding. Is the time here when Pygmies are too cobby and compact to kid without surgical help? When will the time come when Nigerian Dwarves exceed their height standard and start showing long necks and tiny heads? Breeders of both breeds suggest that Dwarf kids strongly resemble

Hayseed Li'l Turnip, an AGS senior champion Dwarf doe is bred and owned by Lisa Parker.

Pygmies, and that Pygmy yearlings often resemble Dwarves. After those two periods of growth, more diversity between the two breeds is seen.

There is also evidence that differences in temperament exist between the two dwarf breeds in America. Some people say that Nigerians seem to be shyer, less active, and less aggressive than Pygmies. Some say that, even though Dwarves are friendly, they do not calm down quite as quickly as Pygmies. Both breeds make excellent pets.

Production-wise both breeds are similar. Pygmies, if they are not the box-car type some people breed for, give adequate milk (page 16), as do Dwarves. It's been said of Dwarves that they make a good "practice" dairy breed because they dry up so easily that if the owner tires of milking, he can just quit and not feel guilty or compelled to sell the doe. The same can be said of Pygmies, although both breeds would probably feel better if they were relieved during the drying process.

AGS production standards for Dwarves are the same as for Pygmies, one-third the larger breeds, or about 500 pounds per lactation for yearlings.

IDGR has also set production standards for the two breeds. For a silver star, a Pygmy must give 350-459 pounds depending on age or 4.8-5.9% butterfat. For a gold star, Pygmies must give over 460 pounds as a yearling, over 575 pounds between three and seven, and over 460 pounds at age eight, or give 6% butterfat or more.

Nigerian Dwarf does are required to give 410 to 549 pounds or 4.4-5.5% butterfat for a silver star or 550 pounds or more and 5.6% butterfat or more for the gold star.

Pine Cone Valley Ashton, an IDGR Dwarf, bred by Robert Johnson, is the great-grandson of J.J.

Willows April Morning, a Dwarf doe bred by Shaula Parker and owned by Lisa Parker is shown at Heart O' Texas Fair at Waco.

CAN YOU IDENTIFY THE BREEDS?

(1)

(2)

(3)

(4)

(5)

Answers
on
page
140

Bibliography

1. American Goat Society, Inc. *Official Breeders and Judges Training Manual*, and Pygmy Goat Registration Procedures, 1978, Esperance, NY
2. Animal Research Foundation, *Stodghill's Animal Research Magazine*, 43rd edition, Winter, 1974
3. Dairy Goat Journal, *Proceedings of the Third International Conference on Goat Production and Disease*, Jan. 10-15, 1982, Tucson, AZ
4. Gall, Christian, editor, *Goat Production*, Academic Press, 1981
5. Hoversland, Dhindsa, Metcalf; *The Usefulness of the Pygmy Goat as a Research Animal*, 1971, Heart Research Laboratory, University of Oregon medical School, Portland, OR
6. Hall, Alice, *Dairy Goats, Selecting, Fitting, Showing*, 1975, Hall Press
7. International Dairy Goat Registry; "Pygmy and Dwarf Breed Standards"
9. Johnson, Robert; "Is the Nigerian Dwarf a True Breed?"; *Footnotes**
10. Johnson, Robert; "The Nigerian Dwarf Goat," *United Caprine News*, May, 1986
11. Mason, Sandra, and Parker, Shaula; *FOOTNOTES**; Fall, 1989; Spring and Summer, 1990
12. Metcalfe, Hoversland, Erickson, Rogers, Clary, *The Pygmy Goat as an Experimental Animal*, National Academy of SciencesNational Pygmy Goat Association, *Pygmy Goat Memo*, Summer, 1976, Volume 1 Number 2
13. Rogers, Erickson, Hoversland, Metcalfe, Clary, *Management of a Colony of African Pygmy Goats for Biomedical Research*, University of Oregon
14. Individuals:
    Holleran, Betsy--records from Enriquez Herd,
    Maxwell, J. William, reporter--information on early East Coast importations
    Skinner, Dick, stableman--Hearst Castle records
    Grogans--gift of Pygmy pair, 1971

ALSO AVAILABLE FROM

HALL PRESS

P.O. Box 5375
San Bernardino, CA 92412

OTHER GOAT BOOKS

Dairy Goats, Selecting, Fitting, Showing,
by Alice Hall, ISBN 0-932218-01-6, $4.00

Nubian History, America & Great Britain
by Reinhardt, ISBN 0-932218-07-5, $5.50

Fundamentals of Improved Dairy Goat Management
by Dr. R.A. Jackson, ISBN 0-932218-14-8
$7.50

HISTORICAL AUTOBIOGRAPHY

Hindustan as seen by john by John Eby
ISBN 0-932218-05-9 $4.50

Answers to page 138:

1. Gretel, a Pygora doe owned by Laura Beers.
2. 1992 NPGA GCH, Christy Critters Geraldine, 9773F, bred by Christine and Tom Hallquest.
3. AGS Jr. Ch. Dwarf doe, Goodwood Alexandra, bred and owned by Kathy Claps.
4. Hallcienda Julie Esther, a 1992 AGS Pygmy doeling bred and owned by the author.
5. Left, an IDGR Pygmy buck stands downhill from an IDGR Dwarf buck, both owned by Robert Johnson.